The Art of American Whiskey

THE ART OF AMERICAN WHISKEY

A Visual History of the Nation's Most Storied Spirit, through 100 Iconic Labels

»» NOAH ROTHBAUM ««

TEN SPEED PRESS
BERKELEY

»» CONTENTS ««

»» INTRODUCTION «««

Ask just about any drinker—or nondrinker, for that matter—to identify a bottle of Jack Daniel's Tennessee Whiskey on a liquor store shelf. The odds are pretty good that he or she will easily be able to pick out the company's distinctive rectangular bottle and signature black-and-white label—branding that is arguably as familiar as Pepsi's blue-and-red globe, Budweiser's old-timey Gothic lettering, and the Anheuser-Busch seal.

American whiskey is currently having an unprecedented revival: according to the Distilled Spirits Council of the United States (DISCUS), sales of bourbon, Tennessee, rye, and corn whiskey were up nearly 37 percent between 2000 and 2013. Yet when it comes to the subject of American whiskey packaging and design—the beauty and artistry of

its labels, for example—very little has been written or said.

Much of the talk, rightly so, has focused on what is *in* the bottle, and brands have gone to great lengths to highlight their heritage, quality of ingredients, and distilling practices. But there is an equally rich tradition of creating unique and eye-catching branding, which, in my opinion, deserves as much attention and appreciation as any vintage French cognac advertising poster, colorful cigar band, or modern wine label.

When a distillery introduces a new bourbon or rye, ample time goes into the planning of its look and branding strategy. (For example, the label for Jim Beam's Jacob's Ghost White Whiskey not only went through multiple iterations but also required

←«« Whiskey barrels peacefully aging in one of Buffalo Trace's warehouses in Frankfort, Kentucky.

an entirely new printing process to make the oval portrait of the company's founder look right.) If things go well, every store and watering hole will stock the spirit, and its trademark will enter the pantheon of household names, joining all-stars like Wild Turkey, Maker's Mark, and nonliquor standouts like Kleenex and Coca-Cola.

The same was true of the American whiskey market one hundred years ago: it was highly competitive and driven by catchy brand names and memorable label art. While some whiskies from that era survived and still exist today—including Jim Beam, Early Times, the aforementioned Jack Daniel's, and arguably the oldest (and aptly named) Old Overholt, which dates back to 1810—there were also scores of other whiskey brands, big and small, that disappeared over the years.

Many of them were driven out of business by Prohibition and the two world wars. Others were victims of corporate mergers and changing tastes. Historically, it was common for larger distillers to have regional whiskey lines with strong local followings. The same bourbon or rye might have been sold in ten different markets under ten different names. Thanks to the consolidation of producers and distributors, as well as cable, network television, and the Internet's power to shrink the planet, distillers these days focus on building national or international brands. As a result, many of these local brand names have been retired.

Today, the major spirits companies own the intellectual property rights to dozens of dormant whiskies. Every so often, one of these ancient brands is dusted off and resuscitated, like E. H. Taylor, which was reintroduced in 2011, becoming a name once again familiar among drinkers and bartenders. These trademarks are valuable and are often bought or traded by liquor companies. (Sometimes, to keep the rights from expiring, just a single case of alcohol is produced and sold in a sleepy market where it won't get much attention.)

As a whiskey drinker, I long to taste these so-called ghost spirits, which have been off the market for years. (I am not alone—there is an increasingly lucrative market for buying and selling vintage American whiskies, online and at auction.) For reasons of scarcity and finances, my dream will no doubt stay just that; however, I *have* been able to track down some of the historic labels from these long-lost brands. They are thrilling to behold on their own, and I admit to fantasizing about their flavor profiles and pulling together imaginary tasting notes for each one of them.

Most of the art is done in a style that combines regional and folksy iconography with classic industrial design. The spirits companies usually created the art in-house or used local designers. These amazingly colorful and charming labels are often the last links we have to the pioneers of the whiskey industry and are a piece of American history.

Many of these whiskies and their accompanying logos have floated down to us on a grand river of alcohol, passed from one liquor company's portfolio to another. In the process, they tend to lose much of their history and even geographical ties. (For instance, before Prohibition, the mid-Atlantic states were famous for rye whiskey, but those brands either went out business or, like Rittenhouse Rye and Michter's, are now based in Kentucky.) But despite their circuitous paths, they have managed to retain their beauty and capture a real moment in time.

For this book I have chosen labels from brands that are long gone, like O. F. C. and Belle of Lincoln, and also ones from brands that are still with us, like Pappy Van Winkle and Four Roses, as well as new additions to the market. They represent the major periods of American-whiskey history—from its golden age, through Prohibition, and up to the modern craft-distilling boom—and are also a survey of American industrial design. This collection is, of course, the perfect accompaniment to a dram of your favorite whiskey. Cheers!

Ledger 1799

Distillery

Date 1799			Rye Bu:	Corn Bu	Dolls	Cents	Date 1799
Jan.ry 1	To Grain on hand —		250				Jan.ry 7
	" Spirits on hand 60 Gall.s worth 3/6		—		167	50	
to the 31	" Muddy hole this m.o 3/6		—		35	—	12
to do	" Doquurun	do	146		85	16	23 "
	" Daniel M.c Arley	do	84		49		31 "
	" William Violet	do	29		16	92	23 4
	" W.m Tripplet	do	50		29	16	2 1
	" Henry Peake	18	3		1	75	
	" George Gilpin		75	45			
	" Aquil..	31					

1

The LATE 1800s and EARLY 1900s

To talk about the history of American whiskey is to talk about the history of America—it's nearly impossible to untangle the two. While that may sound like hyperbole or typical pub BS, it's actually not too big of an exaggeration.

After all, Scotch, Irish, and German settlers, who brought the art of distillation (and a thirst for spirits) with them from Europe, helped found the country. And after the Revolutionary War, one of the biggest crises the country faced was the Whiskey Rebellion, when the government put down protests in Pennsylvania over newly instituted taxes on distillation. Even our first president, George Washington, can be tied to booze. After leaving office, he built the country's largest rye whiskey distillery on his Virginia estate, Mount Vernon. The facility, which produced eleven thousand gallons of whiskey in 1799, was run by his Scottish plantation manager James Anderson. (It was rebuilt a few years ago, and I'd encourage you to check it out.) Plus, distilling taxes helped fund the Union's Civil War effort.

PREVIOUS PAGE: Production at George Washington's distillery was carefully tracked in the farm's ledger, including the fact that he paid taxes on his whiskey production.

←—« The distillery at Mount Vernon isn't just for display—it is actually used to make whiskey.

The Farm Distiller

Washington was hardly alone. From practically the time colonists first settled America, farms across the United States produced spirits from a range of grains and fruits. Distillers in the mid-Atlantic states and the Northeast traditionally made spicy rye whiskey because the grain, which was prized for its hardiness, was able to survive cold winters. Southern distillers made use of corn—fast growing and sweet—to produce bourbon.

During the second half of the nineteenth century, thanks to distilling and railroad improvements, a number of brands developed dedicated followings and built impressive facilities. Yet in spite of greater distribution, there was still no real branding to speak of. This was largely because, throughout the 1800s, liquor was only sold by the barrel to bars and stores, so consumers usually had access to only a few regional spirits or blends created by wholesalers—whatever they found in the general store or tavern. According to the Kentucky Distillers' Association, the only way to figure out what you were drinking, if you cared, was to look for the name of the distiller or wholesaler, which was burned into the whiskey barrelhead. (Some of the brands did supply branded decanters to bars and stores when they bought a barrel.)

There was one early bourbon pioneer, though: E. H. Taylor, who, according to Michael R. Veach, author of *Kentucky Bourbon Whiskey: An American Heritage*, used shiny brass hoops on his barrels instead of the customary iron or wooden ones to makes sure customers in the 1870s recognized casks of his O. F. C. Whiskey. Taylor seems to be the only one who tried this type of technique.

In 2006 George Washington's distillery at Mount Vernon was rebuilt, complete with working stills. ⟫⟶

Jack Daniel's nephew Lem Motlow filed this trademark application in 1908 for the term "Old No. 7." Nobody's sure why Daniel chose that specific number or phrase, but the whiskey's label still proudly uses it.

A Clear Future

Throughout the nineteenth century, buying whiskey was basically a "self-serve" operation: drinkers could buy a glass of booze at a bar, or they could go to their local grocer or watering hole with an earthenware jug (sometimes branded with a distiller's name), a glass decanter, or a flask, any of which would then be filled from a cask. That all changed in the 1860s when Hiram Walker began bottling his Walker's Club from Ontario, which later became, of course, Canadian Club. Then in 1870, George Garvin Brown and his half brother J. T. S. Brown Jr., the founders of what would turn into Brown-Forman, decided to sell their Old Forester Bourbon (which is still available today) exclusively in glass bottles. They had originally planned to offer it to doctors, who could be sure that the whiskey they were prescribing to patients for a range of health issues was pure and unadulterated.

It was a giant step forward for the industry, since glass bottles allowed drinkers, for the first time, to know without a doubt what they were imbibing. Up until then, there was no telling what you were buying. The bottling trend was helped by the passage of the Bottled-in-Bond Act in 1897 and the Pure Food and Drug Act in 1906, which set up federal regulations about what information was required to be on labels and the veracity of their claims. (A label for Belle of Lincoln Straight Whiskey, which was made by Jack Daniel's and dates from just before 1910, even states that the quality of the liquor is guaranteed under the Pure Food and Drug Act.) What also helped was that, in 1903, Michael J. Owens patented a machine to quickly and cheaply make bottles, and, according to the Kentucky Distillers' Association, it could produce four per second.

The Birth of Branding

Even before bottling became the industry norm, some innovative bourbons were already buying outdoor billboards; in the late 1890s, Four Roses had one on New York's Madison Square. But glass bottles really led to the birth of spirits marketing and branding as we know it.

This evolution was echoed by the broader advertising industry, which took off after the Civil War with the rise of national brands and exploded in the late nineteenth century with advances in lithography and the creation of full-service ad firms.

Starting in the 1880s, spirits companies were advertising in newspapers and magazines as well as creating fanciful labels for their whiskies. According to Veach, these logos soon adorned bar mirrors, drink stirrers, and decanters sold to consumers. In 1908, Jack Daniel's nephew Lem Motlow (who ran the company after his uncle retired) filed a trademark application in Tennessee for the term "Old No. 7," which the brand still uses today on its labels.

The timing couldn't have been more perfect: just as American whiskey was coming into its own as a real business, the aphid-like phylloxera was devouring vineyards across Europe, killing the wine and cognac industries—and creating a world of thirsty drinkers.

The smartest whiskey distillers saw an opportunity to capture new consumers and went to work building up the reputations of their products with sophisticated marketing, which led to the first golden age for the industry.

OLD FORRESTER

Old Forrester, which was introduced in 1870 by George Garvin Brown and his half brother J. T. S. Brown Jr., was the first U.S. brand to come exclusively in a sealed bottle. (The brothers' company would ultimately become Brown-Forman.) This advertisement for the whiskey dates to 1881, when Forester was originally spelled with three *R*s. The ad depicts three monkeys unsuccessfully trying to open the bottle with a corkscrew and, if you will, "monkey around" with the whiskey inside of it, demonstrating the value of the Browns' product.

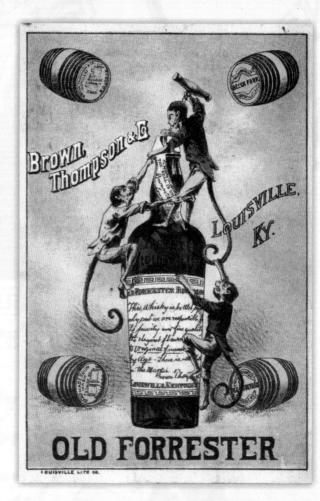

EARLY TIMES OLD STYLE SOUR MASH WHISKEY

Early Times dates back to the 1860s, and this label from 1915 emphasizes the brand's long history and attempt to use historic production methods, which, according to bourbon historian Chuck Cowdery's *Bourbon, Straight: The Uncut and Unfiltered Story of American Whiskey*, included using pot stills instead of popular column stills. Note the distiller listed is J. H. Beam, who was Jim Beam's uncle and founded Early Times when he was just twenty-one.

OLD W. L. WELLER PURE RYE

This ornate rye whiskey label dates from before Prohibition and was used by whiskey wholesaler W. L. Weller & Sons. Julian P. "Pappy" Van Winkle Sr. and his partner later combined the company with the A. Ph. Stitzel Distillery to create the famous Stitzel-Weller Distillery.

GEO. A. DICKEL & CO. CASCADE JUGS

Before distilleries used glass bottles, many of them offered liquor stores branded ceramic jugs that could be filled and sold to customers. This pair, complete with corncob stoppers, comes from George Dickel and was used around 1900. ▶▶→

JACK DANIEL
OLD NO. 7 WHISKEY

While we're used to Jack Daniel's famous black-and-white design, according to legend it wasn't introduced until 1911, after Jack Daniel passed away. Before that historic event, the brand used different labels, including this colorful Art Nouveau design from around 1905.

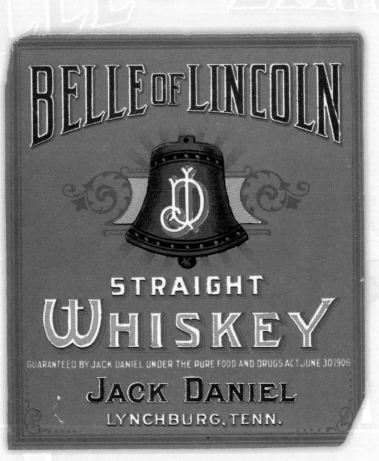

BELLE OF LINCOLN STRAIGHT WHISKEY

GUARANTEED BY JACK DANIEL UNDER THE PURE FOOD AND DRUGS ACT JUNE 30 1906

JACK DANIEL

LYNCHBURG, TENN.

BELLE OF LINCOLN STRAIGHT WHISKEY

Back in the day, Jack Daniel sold whiskey under a second name—Belle of Lincoln. What does Lincoln have to do with bourbon? Well, in this case, we're actually not talking about the president. Lynchburg, Tennessee, where the distillery is still located, was once part of Lincoln County. This ornate label was used around 1910.

JACK DANIELS
NO. 7 WHISKEY

While the United States went dry in 1920, Tennessee passed prohibition legislation in 1909. This label dates from 1910 and was used for the only type of alcohol still available in the state: so-called medicinal whiskey, which you could only purchase from a pharmacy with a prescription from a doctor or dentist. It was most likely created by a Nashville distributor, which is why the apostrophe is missing from the brand's name.

GEO. A. DICKEL & CO.
CASCADE KENTUCKY STRAIGHT
BOURBON WHISKY

Thanks to Tennessee's prohibition, Dickel was forced to close down its Cascade Distillery in Tullahoma. To keep whiskey on the shelves, the brand had Louisville-based A. Ph. Stitzel produce and bottle its bourbon.

OLD HICKORY O. P. S. RYE WHISKEY

This stately label from 1903 befits its namesake, former president, war hero, and famous Tennessee resident Andrew Jackson. (He also had a distillery at his plantation, the Hermitage, outside of Nashville.) It bears his portrait and makes use of his nickname, Old Hickory.

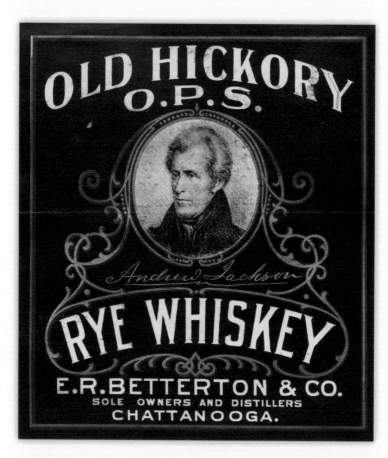

REGISTERED U.S. PATENT OFFICE.

T.W. SAMUELS

BOTTLED IN BOND

WHISKEY

RICH AND MELLOW AGED IN WOOD

By *S.H. Samuels* Distiller.

ESTABLISHED IN 1844.

T. W. SAMUELS BOTTLED IN BOND WHISKEY

While the Samuels are now famous for starting Maker's Mark in the 1950s, the family's original brand was T. W. Samuels. This label from the early 1900s for the bottled-in-bond whiskey almost looks like it could be on a mirror behind a turn-of-the-century bar.

COCKTAILS OF THE TIME

During the 1800s, cognac was king, and many drinks, including the Mint Julep, called for the grape-based brandy. But when the phylloxera epidemic decimated European grape vines, cognac production was temporarily halted, and bartenders and drinkers were forced to use the era's other two popular spirits—gin and whiskey—even more in their cocktails. Try New York Distilling Company cofounder and all-star bartender Allen Katz's delicious recipes for the classic Sazerac, Mint Julep, and Bourbon Rickey, and you'll understand why cognac was never able to regain its title.

SAZERAC

CONTRIBUTED BY ALLEN KATZ

Herbsaint or absinthe
1 sugar cube
2½ ounces American rye whiskey
1 dash Angostura Bitters
2 dashes Peychaud's Bitters
GARNISH: Lemon twist
GLASS: Old-fashioned

»»» Rinse an old-fashioned glass with Herbsaint or absinthe so that the glass is well coated. Discard any excess and set the glass aside. In a mixing glass, muddle the sugar cube with a few drops of water. Add the rye and bitters, fill the mixing glass with ice, and stir until chilled. Strain into the Herbsaint-rinsed glass and garnish with the lemon twist.

MINT JULEP

CONTRIBUTED BY ALLEN KATZ

8 fresh mint leaves

1 teaspoon granulated sugar

2½ ounces bourbon

GARNISH: Sprig of fresh mint

GLASS: Julep cup

⏵⏵⏵ Put the mint, sugar, and a small amount of crushed ice in a julep cup and muddle. Add more crushed ice to half fill the cup, and then add the bourbon. Stir until the drink is well chilled and the cup becomes frosty. Add more crushed ice to fill the cup, garnish with the mint sprig, and serve with straw.

BOURBON RICKEY

CONTRIBUTED BY ALLEN KATZ

½ lime

2 ounces bourbon

Chilled club soda

GLASS: Collins

⏵⏵⏵ Squeeze the lime into a Collins glass filled with ice. Add the bourbon and the spent lime shell and top with club soda.

2

―》》》》》》》― ∙ ―《《《《《《《―

PROHIBITION

―》》》》》》》― ∙ ―《《《《《《《―

Talk about a hangover: drinkers waking up on January 17, 1920, faced a suddenly dry country with a desperate thirst for alcohol.

Thanks to years of work by teetotalers and suffragettes, as well as World War I (which stirred up anti-German and antibeer sentiment), America was out of the spirits business and for the next thirteen years would suffer under the vagaries of Prohibition. Buying a cocktail, a dram, or a beer now meant breaking the law and possibly drinking a beverage of dubious origin. The Great Experiment, as the period was called, also enriched the Mob, ruined the legitimate profession of bartending, and corrupted officials on all levels. As if that wasn't bad enough, to make up for all the taxes that the liquor industry had been contributing to federal coffers, Congress instituted a personal income tax, which we all still pay today.

It was enough to drive you to drink.

PREVIOUS PAGE: Deputy New York police commissioner John A. Leach makes sure a confiscated barrel is disposed of.

◄—◄◄ A sad end for cases and cases of confiscated illegal liquor.

The Volstead Act, which was the legislative backbone of Prohibition, shut down all the country's distilleries except for six, which were allowed to sell only "medicinal" spirits: the Brown-Forman Distillery Company, Frankfort Distilleries Inc., James Thompson and Brother (which soon became Glenmore Distilleries Co.), the American Medicinal Spirits Company, the Schenley Distillers Corporation, and the A. Ph. Stitzel Distillery. These companies were lucky compared to, say, Jim Beam and his family, who were forced into the stone quarry business to keep afloat during Prohibition.

A Whiskey Cure-All

The six brands that could operate during Prohibition were not allowed to distill new whiskey, though they could sell off their existing stock. These companies were also forced to adhere to the strict rules of the "medicinal" whiskey game: The liquor had to be 100 proof, aged in bonded warehouses, and sold mostly

A 1923 raid of the Lunch Room nets D.C. Prohibition officers a trove of alcohol.

in pints or sometimes half-pints. They could also sell whiskey on behalf of other distillers. "They charged a storage fee and a bottling fee, plus a small commission," says historian Michael R. Veach.

While the only people who could legally buy liquor were doctors, dentists, pharmacists, bakers, and individuals with a prescription from an MD, the operational brands still sold plenty of alcohol. (By 1925, the George T.

A moonshining operation was discovered in Washington, D.C. in 1922. It was, according to the image's caption, the largest still yet to be found at the time.

←—◀◀ A keg of beer is emptied by Philadelphia public safety director Smedley D. "Duckboards" Butler.

Stagg Distillery had bottled one million pints of medicinal whiskey.)

Why the success? It was largely the number of scripts written by doctors for a range of "maladies" that could, of course, be cured by a healthy jigger. According to DISCUS, about ten thousand prescriptions were issued to Nevada's population of roughly ninety thousand people in just one year of Prohibition.

So much liquor was sold, in fact, that the companies began to run low on whiskey, which started a wave of mergers and acquisitions. Brown-Forman bought historic bourbon producer Early Times in 1923 to get access to its whiskey. Ultimately, the government allowed the distilleries to make more medicinal alcohol for one hundred days in 1929, during which three million gallons of liquor was produced at the few remaining functioning distilleries.

The Battle for the Medicine Chest

You might assume that the medicinal booze was sold in nondescript bottles, like those used for rubbing alcohol or penicillin pills. But, as in other eras, packaging, labeling, and branding were important. Companies went to great lengths to differentiate the medical spirits available.

The government did require that the liquor come in special tin-capped pints that were then packed in cardboard boxes. These special bottles were, according to Veach, "developed in Canada because the Canadian whisky distillers found that there was less breakage in smuggling them into the United States. The Prohibition officials thought they also added more security to the bottles and prevented tampering so they insisted that the companies selling medicinal spirits use them here as well." The brands didn't let the advertising opportunity go to waste and covered the boxes and bottles with graphics, logos, and slogans. Old Barbee Whiskey, the self-proclaimed "nonpareil of American whiskies," even stated on its highly decorative box that it was the "best for the medicine chest."

ECHO SPRING WHISKEY

While Echo Spring Bourbon is still produced, it's relatively hard to find. But back in the day, it was very well-known—even mentioned several times in Tennessee Williams's famous play *Cat on a Hot Tin Roof*. The label features a Davy Crockett–like frontiersman listening for (I imagine) the echo.

FOUR ROSES

Fans of historic Four Roses would be sure to spot this ornate box decorated with its signature flowers on the pharmacy shelf. This particular bottle was prescribed to a patient in Sparks, Nevada, in 1924. According to the label, two ounces of whiskey were to be mixed with hot water.

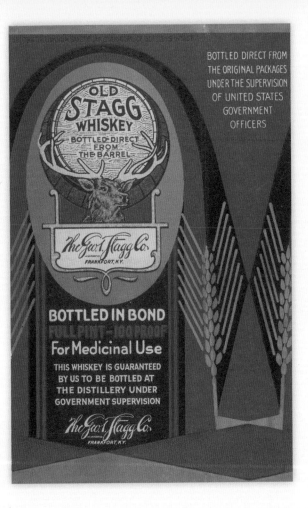

OLD STAGG WHISKEY

The highly stylized packaging for this sixteen-year-old whiskey is one of my all-time favorites and features Art Deco elements, including the modern wheat sheaves as well as more traditional type fonts like the one used for the name of the distillery.

O. F. C. WHISKEY

O. F. C. was founded by bourbon legend E. H. Taylor. During Prohibition, pints of it were packed in this purple-and-yellow box, which features endorsements from the "leading chemists" of the time.

O.F.C. WHISKEY BOTTLED IN BOND FULL PINT 100 PROOF FOR MEDICINAL USE

THIS WHISKEY IS GUARANTEED BY US TO BE BOTTLED AT THE DISTILLERY UNDER GOVERNMENT SUPERVISION

The Geo. T. Stagg Co. FRANKFORT, KY.

THE LEADING CHEMISTS SAY

"A perfect distillation from Grain"

"Not to be improved upon in purity or cleanliness of manufacture."

"I recommend it to the Public, and to the Medical Profession in their practice."

O. F. C.

AFFIX Rx LABEL

THROUGH OPENING

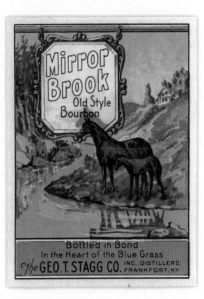

MIRROR BROOK OLD STYLE BOURBON

If the horses didn't tip you off, the label and box for Mirror Brook Old Style Bourbon indicate that it hails from the "Heart of the Blue Grass" (Kentucky's two pastimes, of course, being racing horses and making whiskey). The pastoral scene, complete with a mansion in the distance, seems to play to drinkers' sense of nostalgia.

GOLDEN WEDDING BRAND RYE WHISKEY

Without even opening the box, "patients" could see an image of the ornate "Bell Design Pinch Bottle," which Golden Wedding introduced on December 31, 1924. The packaging seems oddly celebratory—including the ringing church bells embossed into the bottle—for a whiskey that was supposedly for medicinal use.

STAGG'S ELKHORN OLD STYLE KENTUCKY WHISKEY

From the color palette to the idyllic scene to the painting technique, you could easily mistake this label for a vintage 1930s poster advertising train travel.

OLD FASHIONED MOUNTAIN CORN WHISKEY

The label for this sixteen-year-old whiskey combines an idyllic
watercolor scene featuring a stand of corn stalks with an
impressive gold seal adorned with, naturally, ears of corn. The
seal looks like something you might find on the walls of New
York's monument to Art Deco design, Rockefeller Center.

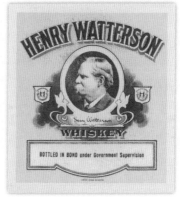

HENRY WATTERSON WHISKEY

Most drinkers would have been quite familiar with Henry Watterson, who was not only the Pulitzer Prize–winning editor of the well-regarded *Louisville Courier-Journal*, but also a staunch critic of Prohibition.

OLD KING COLE WHISKEY

A brand using a nursery school rhyme as its name—and bottle art featuring kids—would certainly not be approved today, but doctors could prescribe this fancifully packaged whiskey to patients during Prohibition.

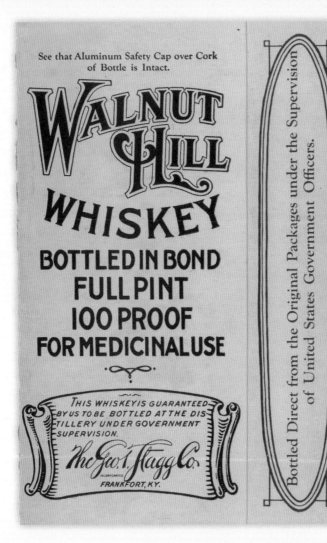

See that Aluminum Safety Cap over Cork of Bottle is Intact.

WALNUT HILL WHISKEY

BOTTLED IN BOND
FULL PINT
100 PROOF
FOR MEDICINAL USE

THIS WHISKEY IS GUARANTEED BY US TO BE BOTTLED AT THE DISTILLERY UNDER GOVERNMENT SUPERVISION.

The Geo. T. Stagg Co.
INCORPORATED
FRANKFORT, KY.

Bottled Direct from the Original Packages under the Supervision of United States Government Officers.

WALNUT HILL WHISKEY

It would be practically unpatriotic not to drink Walnut Hill Whiskey, which features a throwback-style label with Uncle Sam in his red-white-and-blue finest.

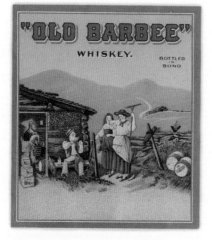

OLD BARBEE WHISKEY

Old Barbee's box makes its case immediately, calling itself the "best for the medicine chest" and "the Nonpareil of American Whiskies." Meanwhile, the label takes a more folksy approach with what looks to be a rural, family-run distillery.

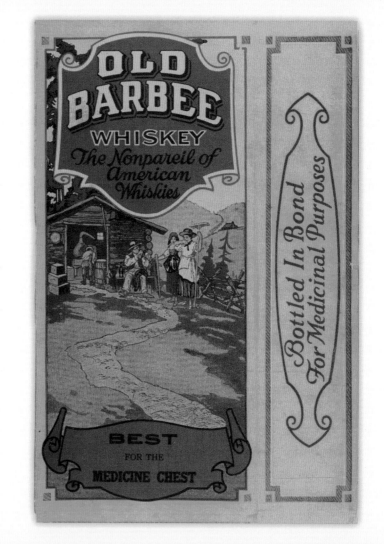

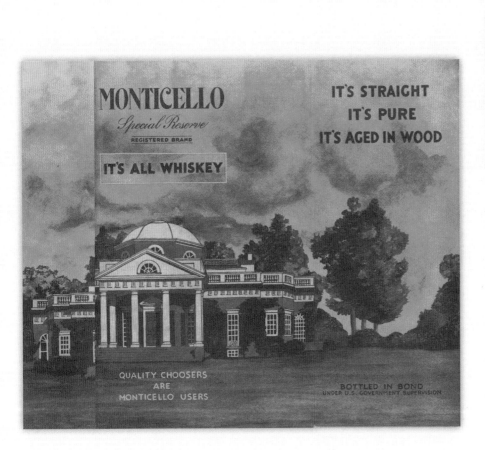

MONTICELLO SPECIAL RESERVE RYE WHISKEY

Before Prohibition, the mid-Atlantic states were famous for their rye whiskies, including the Monticello Distillery in Baltimore. Noted journalist H. L. Mencken mentioned his father drinking the brand in his autobiography *Happy Days*. In the 1880s, he said, locals "drank straight whiskey straight, disdaining both diluents and chasers."

COCKTAILS OF THE TIME

Contrary to popular belief—and the current romanticizing of speakeasy culture—Prohibition was actually a terrible time to be a drinker. The liquor was at best just barely drinkable, and cocktails were made to be downed quickly given that a raid could happen at any moment. (Ginger Ale Highballs—a mix of whiskey and, of course, ginger ale—were popular.) It's likely that people began making the Old-Fashioned with muddled fruit during this dry period to cover up the taste of bad whiskey. One of the few delicious cocktails to be born during Prohibition, according to Gary Regan, author of *The Bartender's Bible* and *The Joy of Mixology*, was the Scofflaw, which was actually dreamed up in Paris. Whatever its origins, it's still a great drink.

OLD-FASHIONED

CONTRIBUTED BY GARY REGAN

  1 sugar cube
  3 dashes Angostura Bitters
  1 orange twist
  3 ounces bourbon or straight rye whiskey
  GARNISH: Orange twist
  GLASS: Old-fashioned

>>> Muddle the sugar cube, bitters, and orange twist in an old-fashioned glass. Fill with ice and add the whiskey. Garnish with the orange twist and stir.

SCOFFLAW COCKTAIL

CONTRIBUTED BY GARY REGAN

  2 ounces bourbon or straight rye whiskey
  1 ounce dry vermouth
  ¼ ounce fresh lemon juice
  ½ ounce grenadine
  2 dashes orange bitters
  GLASS: Cocktail

>>> Put all the ingredients in a shaker and fill with ice. Shake and then strain into a chilled cocktail glass.

3

LIFE after TEMPERANCE

The United States hit rock bottom in 1933. At the worst depths of the Great Depression, roughly a quarter of the country's population was left unemployed, according to the U.S. Department of Labor. And many of those who were lucky enough to have jobs were only working part-time.

At that point, it was hard to deny that Prohibition was a colossal mistake. Shutting down distilleries, breweries, bars, and all the ancillary businesses that they supported was no longer justifiable. That's not even to mention the crime, corruption, and extreme violence caused by bootlegging.

On February 20, 1933, Congress passed the Twenty-First Amendment to the Constitution, which repealed the Eighteenth Amendment (which had, of course, outlawed the manufacture, sale, and transportation of alcohol). Before the Twenty-First Amendment could be added to the Constitution, it needed to be ratified

PREVIOUS PAGE: A view of the ornate Four Roses Distillery from right after the repeal of Prohibition, when it was called the Old Joe Distillery.

←◄◄ A view of the George T. Stagg distillery (now called Buffalo Trace) in Frankfort, Kentucky, at the end of Prohibition in 1933. It was one of the lucky facilities to stay in business during the dry period.

by at least three-quarters of the states. On December 5, at exactly 5:31 p.m. Eastern time—a moment every drinker should remember and toast annually—Utah, the thirty-sixth and final state needed to ratify the amendment, agreed to its terms. Prohibition was finally over.

Delayed Satisfaction

But celebrating the news with a proper and legal drink wasn't that easy. Before stores and bars could begin selling alcohol, each state had to first enact its own liquor laws, and on December 5, according to the Associated Press, only thirteen states were allowing booze to be poured. On Repeal night, the *New York Times* checked in on some of the Big Apple's famed restaurants and hotels (drinking in bars wasn't legal just yet in the state of New York). A few establishments had remarkably managed to get liquor deliveries (from trucks secured with armed guards) as soon as the amendment was ratified. Others had been secretly stocking up on medicinal

whiskey in hopes of a repeal, and still others dug out wines and spirits that dated back to before the start of Prohibition.

Some establishments that couldn't get liquor from legal distributors or had no stocks of their own were forced, according to the *Times*, to buy booze from what the paper called "reliable speakeasies" that had a selection that could be trusted to be potable. This wasn't a problem, since not surprisingly, "the midtown speakeasies were dead. Most of them were deserted by their customers, who went out to try the novelty of drinking in the open."

The market was quickly flooded with alcohol from Europe (some brought over immediately via cruise ships), cheap West Indian rum, and whisky manufactured in Canada. (Schenley's best seller, Ancient Age whisky, was produced across the border.) In American distilleries, whatever bourbon and rye that *hadn't* been sold as medicinal whiskey was finally bottled and sold. And since production had essentially halted for almost all of the thirteen years of Prohibition, it was common to find a selection of sixteen-year-old bourbons and ryes. (A price list from October 1, 1935, published by the Washington State Liquor Control Board, which controlled the types of alcohol available in the state and how much the bottlings could be sold for, includes seven of these mature bottlings.) But after years of aging in barrels, many of these older spirits were, sadly, quite woody and tough to drink.

Back to Work

But with Repeal, distillers were finally allowed to get back to work. In the first twelve months, according to the *Times*, 150 distilleries were opened, with another 200 in the works. Most of the existing pre-Prohibition facilities, according to Chuck Cowdery's *Bourbon, Straight: The Uncut and Unfiltered Story of American Whiskey*, needed to be completely rebuilt since many had been stripped of any valuable machinery or metals or had been left dormant for years. During the lean Prohibition

years and even after Repeal, thanks to the high cost of starting up, many bourbon companies went out of business—and a number of the brands along with their trademarks were picked up by large players on the scene, such as Old Crow, I. W. Harper, and George A. Dickel's Cascade Whisky.

However, those distilleries that could stay in business benefited from a surge in consumer interest. When Jim Beam requested a distilling permit from the Bureau of Industrial Alcohol on December 7, 1933, he stated that his company had a "daily capacity of six hundred bushels, producing approximately three thousand gallons of Bourbon whiskey."

In 1933, Lehman Brothers helped the country's second-largest whiskey producer, Schenley Distillers, with a public offering of shares valued at $3 million. According to papers in Harvard Business School's Lehman Brothers Collection, Schenley had sales of $40.3 million and earnings of $6.9 million in 1934, which grew to $63 million and $8 million, respectively, in 1935. Glass manufacturers also reportedly had trouble keeping up with demand for whiskey, cocktail, and champagne glassware.

As a result of this boom, drinkers could find a range of relatively young whiskies on store shelves by the end of the decade. And brands became ever more creative in marketing these spirits. On September 11, 1937, the *New Yorker* ran an item about a new patent for a process that used sound waves to supposedly speed up the aging of liquor—an unconventional approach that some modern-day craft distillers who are also trying to rush their products to store shelves have actually embraced today.

The bourbon companies were, of course, trying to reclaim their former customers and reach new ones with flashy advertising and bottle designs. In 1934, the whiskey-based liqueur Southern Comfort introduced a fluted bottle with a label featuring a Currier & Ives illustration of a Mississippi River scene. Four Roses Bourbon went so far as to erect a giant neon sign at the northern end of New York's Times Square in 1938, which was so bright and large it could be seen from the Statue of Liberty. And according to Bernie Lubbers's *Bourbon Whiskey: Our Native Spirit*, in 1939, National Distillers replaced a drawing of bourbon legend Basil Hayden on its Old Grand-Dad label with a picture of an actual bust that it had had carved by an artist.

Not only did these packaging upgrades grab attention, but they also allowed the distillers to distance themselves from the low-grade and often dangerous products sold by bootleggers during Prohibition. The new branding signaled to the world that once again the American whiskey industry was open for business!

BOURBON FALLS KENTUCKY STRAIGHT BOURBON WHISKEY

Bourbon Falls was the first whiskey sold by Heaven Hill, which started up right after the end of Prohibition. This striking Art Deco label was used in the late 1930s.

OLD POLK BRAND KENTUCKY STRAIGHT BOURBON WHISKY

This no-frills whiskey pint label features a portrait of its namesake, President James K. Polk. Ironically enough, while he was in office, Polk's wife banned hard alcohol from the White House.

· BROWN·FORMAN ·

Old Polk
Brand

100 PROOF · 100 PROOF

ONE PINT

KENTUCKY STRAIGHT BOURBON WHISKY

DISTILLED AND BOTTLED BY BROWN-FORMAN DISTILLERY CO., INC., AT LOUISVILLE IN KENTUCKY

REG. U. S. PAT. OFF.

· KENTUCKY ·

**OLD FORMAN BRAND
AMERICAN TYPE STRAIGHT
BOURBON WHISKY**

Old Forman tried to appeal to drinkers'
nostalgia with this pastoral (and almost
sepia-toned) image of a farm.

FOUR ROSES 1934 ADVERTISEMENT

In this advertisement from 1934, Four Roses touts not only the quality of its liquor ("blended with the finest whiskies, aged by Father Time himself in charred oak barrels") but also the quality of its bottle "that makes tampering or adulteration impossible." Both were real concerns for drinkers right after Prohibition.

FOUR ROSES 1941 ADVERTISEMENT

With Prohibition having ended several years before, the brands were finally able to start introducing some whiskies that were fully mature. This advertisement is for the Four Roses special 1941 bottling, which was aged for at least five years and came in a fancy bottle. ▶▶▶→

BOTTLED IN BOND OLD RIP VAN WINKLE KENTUCKY STRAIGHT BOURBON WHISKEY

A Moses-like portrait of folk legend Rip Van Winkle leaving the forest would have attracted the eye and conveyed to drinkers that the whiskey too had been lying down for years. (Since it was bottled in bond, we know the liquor by law was at least four years old and 100 proof.) The brand was resurrected in the 1970s and is still available today.

HEAVEN HILL ARTIST RENDERINGS

The first step in creating a label is, of course, to hire a graphic designer to produce a mock-up. While that art is now generally made on a computer, back in the day artists would do it the old-fashioned way: by hand. Heaven Hill Distilleries has a collection of amazing artists' renderings, which were dreamed up sometime between its founding after Prohibition and 1946. While these concepts are quite striking, the company isn't sure if they were ever used.

Even after Repeal, the speakeasy left a lasting imprint on American culture. One effect, according to cocktail historian David Wondrich, is that it became acceptable for women to have a tipple in bars. But the quality of the whiskey available was spotty to say the least. So it's no surprise that a number of the popular whiskey cocktails of the time call for a range of flavorful ingredients to cover up the taste of young whiskey. They also became popular among the new female bar patrons, for whom an order of straight whiskey wasn't an option.

WARD EIGHT

CONTRIBUTED BY DAVID WONDRICH

2 ounces straight rye whiskey
½ ounce fresh lemon juice
¼ ounce fresh orange juice
¼ ounce grenadine (or more, to taste)
Sparkling water
GLASS: Goblet (8-ounce)

➤➤➤ Put all the ingredients except the sparkling water in a shaker and fill with ice. Shake well and strain into a stemmed 8-ounce goblet. Add one ice cube and a splash of sparkling water.

FRISCO COCKTAIL

CONTRIBUTED BY DAVID WONDRICH

2¼ ounces straight rye or bourbon whiskey
¾ ounce Bénédictine
Thin-cut lemon peel
GLASS: Cocktail

>>> Put all the ingredients except the lemon peel in a shaker and fill with ice. Shake well and strain into a chilled cocktail glass. Twist the lemon peel over the top to express the oils, and then discard the peel.

VIEUX CARRÉ

CONTRIBUTED BY DAVID WONDRICH

1 ounce straight rye whiskey
1 ounce VSOP-grade cognac
1 ounce Italian red vermouth
1 teaspoon Bénédictine
1 dash Angostura Bitters
1 dash Peychaud's Bitters
Thin-cut lemon peel
GLASS: Cocktail

>>> Put all the ingredients except the lemon peel in a mixing glass and fill with cracked ice. Stir well and strain into a chilled cocktail glass. Twist the lemon peel over the top to express the oils, and then discard the peel.

The SHAPIRA FAMILY

Families built the American whiskey industry. Some of them are now famous, like the Beams, the Daniels, and the Van Winkles; others are less well-known but no less important, including the Russells (of Wild Turkey) and the Samuelses (of Maker's Mark). While they all tend to have interesting histories, the Shapira clan has one of the most fascinating stories.

The family is a relative newcomer to the industry—opening Heaven Hill Distilleries in Bardstown, Kentucky, in 1934—especially considering that many other brands have lineages that stretch back several centuries. Max Shapira and his five sons, Ed, Gary, George, David, and Mose, can thank Prohibition and the Great Depression for their start.

When the Eighteenth Amendment was repealed in 1933, the whiskey industry was in tatters, with more than half the brands out of business and others forced to completely rebuild their distilleries. Even worse, banks were still wary of the liquor trade and reticent to support it with loans. Most distillers were forced to find outside investors to get their operations going.

While the Shapiras didn't know anything about distilling, they were born salespeople. Max had emigrated to America from Lithuania in the late 1800s along with droves of other Eastern European Jews fleeing pogroms and looking for new opportunities. "Like so many other individuals of that era, he was a peddler and started off with a large pack on his back," says his grandson, Max L. Shapira, who is the president of Heaven Hill today. The elder Max sold notions, including buttons and threads, and then began selling clothes. He was successful enough that he moved up to a horse-drawn carriage and went from town to town hawking dry goods. Ultimately, he settled in New Haven, Kentucky (about ten miles from Bardstown), and founded the

Louisville Stores, which sold men's and women's clothing. "As the sons came of age, they were sent out to open dry goods stores in other small towns in the state of Kentucky," says Shapira.

Despite the country being in the throes of the Great Depression, the family was not only able to keep their stores open, but "business actually prospered," says Shapira. "People even in the Depression needed socks for ten cents a pair." The money that they were able to make during this period "was the genesis of this enterprise" he says.

After Prohibition fell, "quite a number of people were interested in opening a distillery," says Shapira, and were looking for investors. "It was private equity, 1930s-style."

Barely a year after Repeal, the family put up $15,000 and joined a group of partners with distilling knowledge to found Old Heavenhill Springs. (The name would later be changed.) At the time, it took guts to make an investment given that they were creating a brand from scratch and had no inventory

to sell or income coming in, and that the Depression was raging on.

It took just a year to get up and running, and on Friday, December 13, 1935, the first barrel of bourbon was filled. At the beginning the Shapiras got by selling Bourbon Falls Whiskey, a two-year-old bourbon. But the company's first big success was the four-year-old, 100-proof Old Heaven Hill bottled-in-bond bourbon. "That's what everybody wanted," says Shapira. "Quickly the Old Heaven Hill brand became the largest-selling whiskey in Kentucky."

Around that time, the Shapira clan spent another $17,000 to buy out their partners. They continue to run the company today and remain proudly independent. It's quite a feat, given that most of the big American whiskey companies have been bought and sold several times and are now generally part of international conglomerates. Heaven Hill is the largest family owned and operated independent spirits company in the United States.

OLD HEAVEN HILL SPRINGS DISTILLERY. INC.
BARDSTOWN - NELSON COUNTY. KY.

In 1946, after World War II ended, the Shapiras hired Earl Beam, Jim Beam's nephew, to be their master distiller. (He replaced his cousin Harry Beam.) Earl's son, Parker, and his grandson, Craig, are Heaven Hill's master distillers today, and the Beams helped the company become a whiskey powerhouse: since Prohibition, it has filled more than six million barrels of bourbon and currently has an inventory of more than nine hundred thousand barrels.

While Heaven Hill itself isn't a household name, its Evan Williams, Elijah Craig, Old Fitzgerald, and Rittenhouse Rye brands are well-known. The company now sells more than a dozen different whiskies.

In 2004, Heaven Hill opened the Bourbon Heritage Center, which is one of the main attractions on the Bourbon Trail. And in the fall of 2013, it debuted the Evan Williams Bourbon Experience in downtown Louisville, which includes a still and exhibits.

THE WILLETT DISTILLING COMPANY.
NO. 43 BARDSTOWN, NELSON COUNTY, KY.

41384
C
D 160 P

O.P.G.4769   BOURBON WHISKEY

O.P.105   SERIAL NO.

O.T.83   FILLED MAY 27 1950

4

G.I. JOE and the MAN
in the GRAY FLANNEL SUIT

J ust as America was getting accustomed to being a nation of drinkers and the spirits industry was producing whiskey again, the unthinkable happened: Japan attacked Pearl Harbor on December 7, 1941, and the United States entered World War II.

So what did that mean for distillers? To support the war effort, liquor was taxed at unprecedented levels, and most of the country's distilleries were forced by the government to produce high-proof alcohol used to make necessities such as explosives, rubber, and antifreeze. When the measures were enacted, the War Production Board (WPB) was quick to promise the public that this wasn't an attempt to restart Prohibition. In fact, the WPB calculated that the county had a stock of 550 million gallons of whiskey at the beginning of the war, which would last four or five years based on annual consumption rates. This supply was particularly important, since as the fighting got worse, shipments of Scotch and other European spirits became increasingly rare.

PREVIOUS PAGE: A barrel of Willett Bourbon awaits racking.

←—« In 1953, the George T. Stagg Distillery filled its two-millionth barrel since Prohibition, which was proudly displayed in a special warehouse constructed for the occasion. Whiskey pioneer Albert Blanton (in the tie, third from the left) looks at the cask approvingly.

The war effort required the stills to run twenty-four hours a day, seven days a week. And according to historian Veach, with many of the distillery men fighting across Europe and Asia, women and African-Americans went to work in the business for the first time.

A Wartime Thirst

As the war raged, it got harder and harder to get a bottle of whiskey in America, and many states instituted a system of rationing. It was so difficult, in fact, that bootleggers came out of retirement and a black market sprung up for booze. Profiteering distributors also dreamed up all kinds of schemes to make stores pay as much as possible for a case of whiskey. As a result, almost two years after Pearl Harbor, the *New York Times* reported that twelve thousand liquor stores around the country had already gone out of business, with more expected to give up their licenses.

On the war front, G.I.s were dispatched around the globe, and while they could get some American whiskey, it was usually of very low quality. So it's no shock that they developed a taste for rum (usually mixed with some ubiquitous and inexpensive Coca-Cola), French wines, cognac, or smooth blended Scotch.

A New World

When the soldiers returned home, the world was, of course, a very different place. For one, the mid-Atlantic states would never again be the center of rye whiskey production. Before World War I, "if it didn't say Pennsylvania or Maryland, people didn't think it was really rye," remembers Jimmy Russell, Wild Turkey's long-serving master distiller and American whiskey legend. But Prohibition, both world wars, and the G.I. Bill–fueled housing boom doomed the business and the local rye-growing farms. Many of the rye brand names were ultimately bought by Kentucky bourbon producers. This is why Heaven Hill now makes Rittenhouse Rye and Pikesville

Supreme Straight Rye, which were originally produced in Pennsylvania and Maryland.

The rest of the whiskey market was also in a pretty shaky state. Bourbon stocks were at very low levels, and it would take several years for mature whiskey to be widely available. It didn't help that prohibitionists, according to Veach, were at first able to limit the amount of grain that distillers could access. As a result, whiskey production after the end of World War II didn't resume until 1946.

Brands did everything they could to get bottles back on the shelves. On February 8, 1947, the *New Yorker* ran a story about the American Distilling Company petitioning the Connecticut Supreme Court to approve its Private Stock Whiskey bottle label. The front label was regal and talked about the history of the brand, but on the smaller label on the back of the bottle was the truth: "Whisky colored and flavored with wood chips. This whisky is less than one month old." The court, fortunately, did not rule in the American Distilling Company's favor.

The Reign of Blends

While distillers were increasing production of straight whiskey, they were still making many cheaper blends that were more profitable, since they could contain younger whiskies and neutral grain spirit. By 1946, according to Wayne Curtis's *And a Bottle of Rum: A History of the World in Ten Cocktails*, sales of blends made up 87 percent of the whiskey market. Seagram even turned the historic and best-selling straight bourbon Four Roses into a cheaper blend in the 1950s.

In the 1958 third edition of *The Fine Art of Mixing Drinks*, author David A. Embury carps about how distillers were manufacturing blended whiskies in the Midwest under their brand names and in some cases turning formerly bonded bourbons (ones that were 100 proof and aged in a bonded warehouse) into blends. "I have never found any blended American whiskey that, to my taste, was even reasonably satisfactory," he wrote.

Distillers also lowered the proof of many 100-proof whiskies to the now-common 86 proof. This, according to Lubbers, was done to make the whiskey more drinkable and to increase profits. Lowering the proof literally means adding more water to the spirit before it's bottled, saving the brand money overnight and increasing supply. (Some brands have gone even further—Jack Daniel's is currently 80 proof, and in 2013, Maker's Mark attempted to lower its proof but was thwarted by a backlash from drinkers.)

In Europe, Scotch distillers were in similarly bad shape. When the war started, "distilling in the UK had barely recovered from the Depression," says Dr. Nick Morgan, Diageo's head of whisky outreach, and things only got worse as the fighting progressed. In 1937, according to Morgan, Scotch distillers produced 24 million gallons of spirit. That number fell to 13.5 million in 1939 and shrank to 1.3 million in 1942. By 1943, thanks to severe barley rationing, the industry was barely making anything and the price of a regular bottle of whisky in British stores nearly doubled, to 25 shillings. These grain restrictions would have been in effect even longer if Winston Churchill hadn't had the foresight to start providing barley to the Scotch industry in 1944, before the fighting was officially finished, to jump-start the country's economy. Thanks to nearly depleted stocks, the brands predicted that rationing of whisky to America would last for five to seven years after the end of the war.

Ironically, while brown-spirit drinkers finally had money to spend on good straight bourbon and rye whiskey for the first time in decades, they mostly had to make do with blends.

The Competition Heats Up

Given these conditions, other spirits categories took off in the late 1940s and early 1950s. In particular, Americans discovered rum and faux-Polynesian tiki drinks, which, thanks to tiki legends Don the Beachcomber and Trader Vic, became a national sensation.

Vodka's popularity also took off in the 1950s, like a space-age rocket ship. Many Americans first tasted the supposedly odorless, colorless, and flavorless spirit in the wildly successful and refreshing Moscow Mule (a simple mix of vodka, ginger beer, and lime juice), which was traditionally served in a sleek copper mug.

But beyond the Hawaiian-shirt-wearing bartenders who worked in the tiki palaces that had opened across the country, the bartending profession couldn't really shake its association with Prohibition-era speakeasies and, worse, the violence of bootleggers. It was no longer an honorable trade, and after so many disruptions, most of the traditional techniques, recipes, and drinks were abandoned in favor of modern mixes, syrups, and shortcuts.

The Spirited Future

Fortunately, the mid- to late 1950s weren't all bad for drinkers. Having survived decades of truly adverse conditions and calamitous disruptions, the bourbon and rye brands finally had up-to-date facilities and were able to focus on distilling whiskey. At the beginning of 1951, the *New York Times* reported that the historic Old Fitzgerald brand had built four new barrel warehouses and had enough capacity to age 200,000 barrels, up from 130,000. Later that year, the company also invested in a direct-mailing campaign that sent five thousand men named Fitzgerald, in ten cities, a letter about their founding family and a Fitzgerald coat of arms.

Not only were there plenty of well-heeled and thirsty Americans, but the U.S. military's suddenly global presence, including its role in the Korean War, also served to introduce bourbon and rye to an international audience. For the first time in quite a while, the future seemed bright for distillers.

MAKER'S MARK
KENTUCKY STRAIGHT
BOURBON WHISKY

Forget fancy design firms: the Maker's
Mark label and bottle were dreamed
up by Margie Samuels, who founded
the brand with her husband, Bill
Samuels Sr. The iconic packaging
has barely changed since it was
introduced in 1958.

OLD POLK BRAND KENTUCKY STRAIGHT BOURBON WHISKY

In the 1930s, Old Polk used a fairly simple label. In the 1940s, it used a full-color and eye-catching one, which included a background of the Capitol and an updated portrait of Polk.

OLD FORMAN BRAND WHISKY—A BLEND

I'd like to imagine that people who drank this whiskey were as dapper as the top-hatted gent featured on the label. The whiskey wasn't straight bourbon or rye but a blend, which was common in the 1940s as brands were struggling to meet demand with so little aged inventory.

ONE PINT

90 PROOF

OLD FORMAN BRAND WHISKY-A BLEND

BLENDED BY
BROWN-FORMAN DISTILLERY Co.
INCORPORATED
AT LOUISVILLE IN KENTUCKY

BOURBON FALLS
KENTUCKY STRAIGHT
BOURBON WHISKEY

From the heavy use of gold to the "seal of acceptance" to the impressive Gothic lettering, this late-1950s label gave an air of quality to Bourbon Falls.

COCKTAILS OF THE TIME

The late 1940s weren't an easy time to be a whiskey drinker, but things got progressively better through the 1950s, with distilleries finally having a chance to produce bourbon and rye. Bartending culture, unfortunately, would take quite a bit longer to recover from the hangover of Prohibition and World War II. Many of the classic cocktails disappeared from bar menus completely. While the "Man in the Gray Flannel Suit" famously sipped icy-cold Martinis and exotic tiki creations, he could still find refreshing Bourbon Highballs and smooth Bourbon Manhattans. Both whiskey drinks still taste good today, especially if you use Jim Meehan's recipes. A stellar bartender and the managing partner of New York's James Beard Award–winning bar PDT (Please Don't Tell), he knows a thing or two about cocktails.

"Two-ingredient cocktails like the Highball require more focus on the glassware, ice, and garnish to complement them," Meehan advises. "Don't ruin a good bourbon with generic ginger ale." And for his Manhattan, "when I forgo rye whiskey for bourbon in a Manhattan, it's typically for a big, bold one like Old Grand-Dad 114."

BOURBON HIGHBALL

CONTRIBUTED BY JIM MEEHAN

2 ounces Woodford Reserve Bourbon

3 ounces Q Ginger (ginger ale)

GARNISH: Vanilla bean, split

GLASS: Collins

⇒⇒⇒ Put a clear ice spear and the bourbon and ginger ale in a chilled Collins glass. Garnish with the vanilla bean near the rim of the glass.

MANHATTAN

CONTRIBUTED BY JIM MEEHAN

2 ounces Old Grand-Dad 114 Barrel Proof Bourbon

1 ounce Martini Rosso Sweet Vermouth

2 dashes Angostura Bitters

GARNISH: Three brandied cherries on a metal pick

GLASS: Coupe

⇒⇒⇒ Put all the ingredients in a mixing glass and fill with ice. Stir and then fine strain into a chilled coupe glass. Garnish with the cherries.

BILL and MARGIE SAMUELS

Why mess with success? Maker's Mark Bourbon's packaging—and whiskey, for that matter—has barely changed since the company produced its first bottles in the fall of 1958.

As a result, Maker's signature sweet, smooth whiskey and its familiar square-based bottle with a hand-dipped red wax seal has become a favorite of drinkers around the world.

While a new whiskey company starting today would certainly hire a design firm to create its logo and branding, Bill Samuels Sr., who founded the bourbon, didn't even need to leave his house—his wife Margie Samuels came up with the name and packaging.

She began working on the design in the basement of their home, displacing her son Bill Samuels Jr.'s photo lab. According to legend, the famous dripping wax was inspired by a collection of old cognac bottles that had been brought back from Europe by relatives. (The wax seal ensured that air wouldn't spoil the liquor.) But Margie wanted more than just a practical seal—she wanted a statement. The only problem was getting the wax to perfectly coat the neck.

Margie was more than up to the challenge, thanks to a degree in chemistry that she earned at the University of Louisville. She took a deep fryer from her kitchen and began experimenting with different formulas of wax. With the help of chemist Tom Hammonds, the brand was able to find the ideal consistency.

She can also be credited with the brand's name. It stems from her "enormous collection of English pewter," says her son, Samuels Jr., and the fact that she was expert on the different maker's marks for each piece. "She liked the name because it came out of her world," he says.

To test out her bottle design, she made one out of papier-mâché. One night at dinner, she showed the mock-up to her husband, the first to see it. Did he like it? "He liked everything but the wax," says Samuels Jr. His father was worried that people wouldn't know how to open the bottle and that each one would have to be hand dipped. But "she insisted on the wax," says Samuels Jr. So for the first year, they attached a small, square "pull me" note to the tab below the cap. The brand removed it once Samuels Sr. was "comfortable a bartender wouldn't go to a butcher's knife to open it." They never did find a way to automate the wax process, and each bottle is hand dipped at the distillery to this day.

Margie's bottle shape proved to be a bit tougher. At the time, there were just a few types of bottles—round and square—and just a handful of differently proportioned cardboard shipping boxes. Margie's innovative design would be a custom order, and given the limited number of bottles the brand would buy, it would be tough to get a glass manufacturer to take on the project. Fortunately, Samuels Sr. knew the CEO of the Owens-Illinois glass company in Toledo, Ohio, and was able to get him on board.

But Owens-Illinois objected to the slight pinch between the shoulder and neck of the bottle that Margie had added, since it would complicate the manufacturing process. Margie stood her ground. "She was unrelenting," says Samuels Jr., since the detail was not only aesthetically important but also responsible for a pleasant gurgle when the bourbon is poured. "She said, you have to go figure it out because we're having it." In the end, the manufacturer caved and the bottle was produced as she envisioned it.

Unfortunately, it wasn't just the bottles that were tough to source. Overall, "it was hard as hell to get supplies," says Samuels Jr. They were forced to print and cut the bourbon's labels on site, which they still do. "We didn't want to be in the label business," admits Samuels Jr.

The finished bottle design, including the old-timey parchment label and the letterpress-like font, was in line with the brand's overall homespun ethos. While the family had at one time owned famed brand T. W. Samuels, Samuels Sr. supposedly perfected the Maker's Mark recipe by baking bread in his kitchen with different ratios of grains that would mimic the spirit's mash bill. (He finally settled on a base for his whiskey of corn, malted barley, and wheat instead of the spicier and more common rye.)

While the family sold the brand to Canadian company Hiram Walker in the early 1980s, and it is now owned by giant Japanese spirits conglomerate Suntory, not much has changed on Star Hill Farm, where the distillery is located. The Samuelses, including third-generation Rob Samuels, have continued to manage the day-to-day operations despite not being the owners.

The brand introduced a second product, Maker's 46, in 2010. While Samuels Jr. did use an outside design firm to create the label and bottle, he first told its staff all about his mother and asked the designers to channel her mind-set. They came back three days later with the packaging, which he loved. "That's what happens when you don't overcomplicate things."

5

The SWINGING SIXTIES

After more than ten years of American prosperity and uninterrupted distilling, things were looking good for the whiskey industry—and the 1960s promised to be great, with President John F. Kennedy's election seemingly ushering in a new, more modern era.

The decade got off to a good start with several European countries, in particular Italy, France, and England, agreeing to end severe restrictions on the importation of American spirits, which opened those markets up for whiskey producers for the first time since before World War II. In 1960, Brown-Forman set a new company record with more than $100 million in net sales, and in 1961, the George T. Stagg Distillery filled its three-millionth barrel since Prohibition.

PREVIOUS PAGE: A conversation in one of Willett's warehouses.

←—« Workers at the Old Prentice Distillery proudly pose with the brand's 300,000th barrel.

Uncle Sam to the Rescue

Thanks to intense lobbying by industry giant Schenley Industries (which owned a number of brands, including I. W. Harper, Ancient Age, Three Feathers, and Old Charter), American whiskey distillers were able to age their products longer—up to twenty years instead of eight—before needing to pay taxes on them. Why the change? Well, Lewis Solon Rosenstiel, Schenley's founder, had bet that the Korean War would drag on and lead to a prolonged interruption in whiskey distilling, like what happened during World War II. In order to have plenty of product to sell and to corner the market, he massively increased the company's production of bourbon. One small problem: The war ended after just three years and there was no shutdown. Rosenstiel was left with plenty of whiskey. After eight years, the bourbon would be considered mature by the government, and Schenley would have had to pay a tax of $10.50 per gallon.

Rosenstiel was able to get the government to change the tax rules with a clause in the Forand Bill, which passed in 1958, just before his tax bill was due. The new legislation covered both future whiskey production and, critically, whiskey in the barrel. While it saved his company a fortune, it also opened the door to distillers creating a range of more mature spirits, which have recently become extremely popular and a lucrative business.

International Distinction

A congressional bill passed in 1964—that for the first time designated bourbon "a distinctive product of the United States and . . . unlike other types of alcoholic beverages, whether foreign or domestic"—helped whiskey distillers further. This provided the liquor protection from international competitors using the term *bourbon* on their labels and gave it a bit of clout—as well as putting it on the same level as France's cognac and Scotland's Scotch.

In the 1960s (as any *Mad Men* fan can tell you) whiskey and other types of liquor flowed freely in bars, homes, and even offices. Hard alcohol was so popular that, according to DISCUS, it stole overall market share from beer during the decade.

National Upheaval

Although the whiskey industry was taking off, the 1960s were far from harmonious, with the country divided on a number of important social and political issues. Kennedy was assassinated in the fall of 1963, and under President Lyndon Johnson, America's role in Vietnam would widen, with troops being officially deployed in 1965. At the same time, the Civil Rights Movement threw the South into a state of upheaval, culminating with the assassination of Martin Luther King Jr. in 1968. The hippies massed in San Francisco for the Summer of Love in 1967, which was followed by the violence of the Democratic National Convention in Chicago the following year and the legendary music festival Woodstock the year after that. The Days of Rage protests closed out the decade, which ultimately would be one of the most cataclysmic and important periods in American history. Bob Dylan, the bard of the 1960s, summed it up best in his song "The Times They Are a-Changin'," which he released in 1964.

The fissure in societal values showed in whiskey label art. During the era, some brands continued to use traditional images that touted their lineage and Southern heritage, while other embraced more modern typefaces and design. This split would widen further during the 1970s.

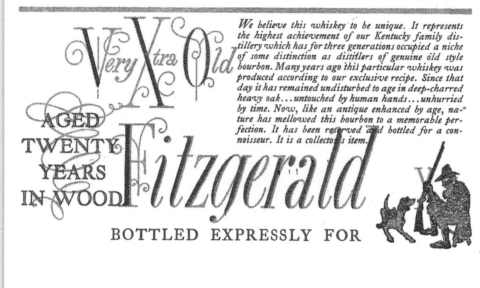

BARRELED IN 1948   RIP VAN WINKLE   BOTTLED IN 1968

Very Xtra Old

AGED
TWENTY
YEARS
IN WOOD

Fitzgerald

BOTTLED EXPRESSLY FOR

We believe this whiskey to be unique. It represents the highest achievement of our Kentucky family distillery which has for three generations occupied a niche of some distinction as distillers of genuine old style bourbon. Many years ago this particular whiskey was produced according to our exclusive recipe. Since that day it has remained undisturbed to age in deep-charred heavy oak...untouched by human hands...unhurried by time. Now, like an antique enhanced by age, nature has mellowed this bourbon to a memorable perfection. It has been reserved and bottled for a connoisseur. It is a collector's item.

VERY XTRA OLD FITZGERALD

Back in 1968, Julian Van Winkle II commissioned this label for a twenty-year-old whiskey. Ultimately he decided not to use it, but the design is quite interesting since it mixes a number of different fonts. The bourbon, which it calls a "collector's item," would have been quite mature and a unique offering for the time.

BOURBON
STAR

KENTUCKY
STRAIGHT BOURBON WHISKEY
86 ● PROOF
Distilled and bottled by
THE WILLETT DISTILLING COMPANY
INCORPORATED
BARDSTOWN · NELSON COUNTY · KENTUCKY
"THIRD GENERATION OF DISTILLERS"

**BOURBON STAR
KENTUCKY STRAIGHT
BOURBON WHISKEY**

This simple but elegant label,
which looks very similar to gas
station signage of the era, was
used by the Willett Distilling
Company for several decades.
While the distillery is still
functioning, this brand is no
longer produced.

DISTILLED IN KENTUCKY

Old Time Sour Mash

CROWN OF NELSON

KENTUCKY
STRAIGHT BOURBON WHISKEY
Distilled and bottled by
THE WILLETT DISTILLING COMPANY
INCORPORATED
BARDSTOWN · NELSON COUNTY · KENTUCKY
"THIRD GENERATION OF DISTILLERS"

CROWN OF NELSON KENTUCKY STRAIGHT BOURBON WHISKEY

The label for Crown of Nelson could easily have been mistaken for an engraved stock certificate. Its stately appearance conveys a sense of quality to drinkers.

CREAM OF NELSON KENTUCKY STRAIGHT BOURBON WHISKEY

Willett made several versions of Cream of Nelson, each with its own parallelogram label.
The whiskey was sold in Japan and several other countries.

BEAM'S PRIVATE STOCK KENTUCKY STRAIGHT BOURBON WHISKEY

Guests staying at La Posada Inn in Santa Fe, New Mexico, could relax by having a glass of the establishment's special four-year-old, 86-proof Jim Beam bourbon. The inn's logo is the epitome of kitschy design—an odd contrast to the label's overall traditional feel.

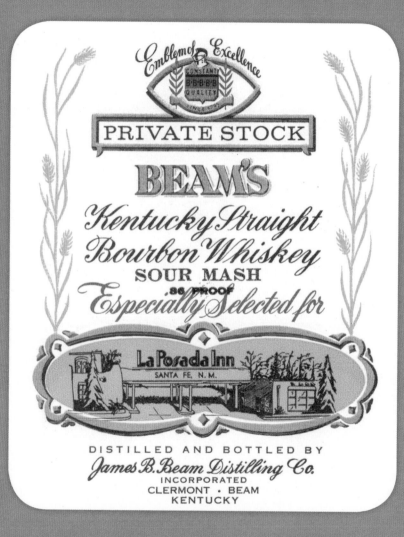

JIM BEAM MANHATTAN COCKTAIL

This 1969 label perfectly encapsulates the progression in liquor packaging design, with a sleek Manhattan cocktail image, gold chain link borders, and modern font, while still paying tribute to the brand's historic roots.

KING KORN
KENTUCKY CORN
WHISKEY

Think white whiskey is hot now? This potent 100-proof corn-based whiskey was aged for one month and was on store shelves in 1969. Its folksy label features an almost cartoonlike font and graphics.

"CORN LIKKER"

PROOF 100 PROOF

KING KORN

KENTUCKY

CORN WHISKEY

BOTTLED BY
THE CLEAR SPRING DISTILLING CO.

CLERMONT, KENTUCKY

DISTILLED IN KENTUCKY

KENTUCKY
NOBLEMAN

43% ALC/VOL (86 PROOF)
KENTUCKY STRAIGHT
BOURBON WHISKEY

Mild and Mellow

BOTTLED IN KENTUCKY BY
KING SPRINGS DISTILLING CO.
Bardstown, Nelson County, Kentucky

KENTUCKY NOBLEMAN
KENTUCKY STRAIGHT
BOURBON WHISKEY

It would be hard to forget where
Kentucky Nobleman was distilled—its
home state is mentioned five times
on the label and is referenced by the
image of a stallion. While the design is
simple, it's quite elegant and conveys
a sense of Southern sophistication.
The brand was primarily sold in just a
few states, including Nebraska.

COCKTAILS OF THE TIME

With the decade's fully stocked office bar carts, boozy lunches, and frequent happy hours, it's no wonder Matthew Weiner set his hit TV show *Mad Men* during the 1960s. And it should come as no surprise that it was a good decade for American, Canadian, and Scottish distillers. Drinkers enjoyed their spirits in a range of cocktails, including the John Collins (a whiskey Tom Collins), the Bourbon Stone Sour, and the Presbyterian. To help you channel your inner Don Draper, enjoy these drink recipes from master mixologist Dale DeGroff, who fathered the rebirth of the cocktail.

PRESBYTERIAN

CONTRIBUTED BY DALE DEGROFF

1½ ounces bourbon or your favorite American whiskey

2½ ounces club soda

2½ ounces ginger ale (or 7UP)

GARNISH: Lemon twist

GLASS: Highball

》》》 Put all the ingredients in a highball glass filled with ice. Garnish with the lemon twist.

BOURBON STONE SOUR

CONTRIBUTED BY DALE DEGROFF

1½ ounces bourbon

¾ ounce simple syrup (a mix of equal parts sugar and water)

¾ ounce fresh lemon juice

1 ounce fresh orange juice

GARNISH: Orange slice and cherry

GLASS: Rocks

➤➤➤ Put all the ingredients in a shaker and fill with ice. Shake and then strain into a rocks glass filled with fresh ice. Garnish with the orange slice and cherry.

JOHN COLLINS

CONTRIBUTED BY DALE DEGROFF

1½ ounces bourbon

¾ ounce simple syrup (a mix of equal parts sugar and water)

¾ ounce fresh lemon juice

1½ ounces club soda

GARNISH: Orange slice and cherry

GLASS: Collins

➤➤➤ Put all the ingredients except the club soda in a shaker and fill with ice. Shake and then strain into a Collins glass filled with fresh ice. Top with the club soda and garnish with the orange slice and cherry.

6

The **SEVENTIES,**
EIGHTIES, and NINETIES,
aka the **DARK AGES**

To paraphrase Charles Dickens, it was the best of times and the worst of times for the American whiskey industry in the 1970s. All-time bourbon sales peaked in 1970, but the brands were beginning to lose ground and control of the market.

After the national upheaval of the 1960s, younger people didn't want to drink like their parents. They wanted something new, something fresh. So it's no surprise that old-timey and traditional spicy rye whiskey almost disappeared completely and American wines started to gain real attention during the decade. The so-called Judgment of Paris on May 24, 1976, in which American wines scored better than French ones in a blind tasting, not only legitimized the movement, but also made California wines instantly famous around the world.

PREVIOUS PAGE: Wild Turkey staff celebrate filling the brand's fifty-thousandth barrel, including bourbon legend-in-the-making Jimmy Russell (standing, in the brown shirt) and Ernest W. Ripy Jr. (kneeling, in the striped shirt), who was the son of one of the distillery's founders.

←◄◄ Fritz Maytag's Anchor Distilling was one of the first craft distilleries in the country.

California would also foster another drinking trend. In San Francisco, Fritz Maytag, who, in 1965, bought the historic and floundering Anchor Steam brewery, embarked on his mission of making beer the old-fashioned way and in the process helped kick off the craft-brewing movement. By 1975, he was bottling traditional brews.

During this period, wine and beer consumption soared. In 1960, according to DISCUS, wine and beer made up 62.2 percent of the alcohol market. By 1990 that share would grow to 70.4 percent. This increase came at the expense of hard spirits sales.

An Invisible Competitor

But American whiskey brands had an even bigger threat looming on the horizon than beer and wine: vodka. The popularity of the supposedly tasteless alcohol had been slowly building in the United States since the 1940s and 1950s but exploded in the 1970s. While vodka made up, according to DISCUS, just 1 percent of all spirits sold in America in 1952, by 1975 the superpopular category would outsell straight and bonded bourbon and rye combined.

Its meteoric rise was helped further by the 1979 introduction of the supercool Swedish brand Absolut, with its sleek modern bottle and later its ingenious ad campaigns featuring work from of-the-moment artists, including Andy Warhol, Keith Haring, and Ed Ruscha. The vodka category never looked back and has been unstoppable ever since. A new king rightfully took its throne.

Whiskey Tries to Go Hip

But the whiskey brands didn't give up without a fight. In the early 1970s, Jim Beam ran a print and billboard advertising campaign targeting baby boomers that matched groovy young stars of the day with older celebrities of the previous generation. One ad featured Orson Welles and his aspiring actress daughter

Rebecca; another, Robert Wagner and Bette Davis; and a third, Dennis Hopper and director John Huston. The tagline for the series was "Generation gap? Jim Beam never heard of it."

Brown-Forman went a step further, introducing a white whiskey in 1971 called Frost 8/80. To create it, the company took an eight-year-old bourbon and filtered out the color and a lot of the flavor. While white whiskey is currently having a moment, Frost 8/80, which reportedly cost millions to develop, was met with a firestorm of criticism from other bourbon distillers. It also failed to entice vodka drinkers back to whiskey and was taken off shelves at the end of 1972.

However, Brown-Forman wasn't the only company to experiment with new product categories. Wild Turkey introduced an 80-proof bourbon-based liqueur in 1976, which the brand's master distiller Jimmy Russell says was an attempt to expand its market and attract female drinkers. At the time, "most ladies felt bourbon was too strong,"

he says. They tried a number of different flavors before deciding on honey, which took a bit of time to catch on. "You never know about these things," he says. A few years later, the company lowered the proof to 60. (It was reintroduced for a second time in 2006 as the 71-proof American Honey, complete with new packaging, and became a best seller—the success of which has led to an array of modern, flavored bourbons and liqueurs.)

The Dark Days

During the rest of the 1970s and through the 1990s, the American whiskey industry suffered a precipitous decline. It faced a range of foreign whiskey rivals, including smooth Canadian whiskies, as well as competition from other categories, including gin and upstarts rum and tequila. This led to a wave of brand consolidations and the closing of a number of distilleries. It was a tough time to be a whiskey drinker.

But you can't have a rebirth without some hard times. Salvation would ultimately come from an unlikely source: Scotland. The country's formidable whisky producers were also at a crossroads, with their U.S. sales reaching an all-time high in 1975 and then declining sharply for the next thirty years.

It got so bad that a number of the Scottish distilleries were mothballed, and economic conditions ultimately forced a major rethinking of the industry's basic business model. Instead of mixing single malts from various distilleries with aged grain whisky to make blended Scotch, the companies began bottling and selling the uncut single malts. These spirits are much more expensive than blends and were marketed as an affordable luxury good for a sophisticated palate, with more flavor and character. Through their packaging and label art, the brands were able to develop unique identities and loyal followings. The blenders followed suit by rolling out more expensive products, like the pricy Johnnie Walker Blue Label.

The Path to Success

New deluxe Scotches also inspired American whiskey companies to introduce their own versions of single malt Scotch—small-batch and single barrel bourbons. In 1984, Elmer T. Lee, master distiller at George T. Stagg, created the world's first single barrel bourbon, Blanton's Single Barrel, which sold for $30, about double the price of a regular bottle of bourbon. "The first year or two . . . they spent more money on advertising than they did on return," recalled Lee in an interview in 2008 for the Bourbon in Kentucky Oral History Project. "But as the word got out and people started trying it, it took a turn up; it's still going up." The owners of the Stagg distillery, according to Lee, even encouraged their competitors to introduce similar whiskies, without much success.

Fortunately, a few years later, in 1988, Jim Beam's master distiller Booker Noe released his Booker's Bourbon, which was joined in 1992 by Baker's, Basil Hayden's, and Knob

Creek to create the Small Batch Bourbon Collection. (You can read more about the creation of these spirits later in this chapter in a profile of Noe; see page 125.) Russell, at Wild Turkey, released his small-batch Rare Breed whiskey in 1991.

What goes better with a glass of fine bourbon than a cigar? In the autumn of 1992, Marvin Shanken launched *Cigar Aficionado* magazine, which celebrated not only stogies but also a new men's lifestyle that included sipping whiskey and other "potions of pleasure," as he called them in his first editor's note. "The whiskey and cigar trends fed off each other," says legendary mixologist Dale DeGroff.

Then in 1993, Fritz Maytag—the man who helped start the craft-beer movement—opened up Anchor Distilling in San Francisco and helped start another trend: craft distilling. He began by making a traditional 100-percent rye whiskey, which was unheard of at the time and a real throwback considering that rye was a dead category. Maytag soon branched out and began making a number of gins, including a Dutch genever-like one whose base was unaged whiskey. And just a few years later and few miles away, Lance Winters began working at St. George Spirits and immediately began producing an American single malt whiskey. The first bottles of it were sold in 2000.

The success of these early efforts and bottlings led many other companies to invest in creating new, higher-priced whiskies, including Brown-Forman's Woodford Reserve, whose distillery in Versailles, Kentucky, opened in 1996.

At the beginning of the new century, American whiskey brands were once again poised for greatness.

BOOKER NOE'S BOURBON

The original small-batch bourbon, Booker's, was introduced in 1988 and set off a bourbon revival. This particular bottle, which was one of the first released, was served at the Oakland Art Novelty Company bar in Ferndale, Michigan. The label features a reproduction of a handwritten note from distiller Booker Noe explaining the story of the whiskey.

ST. GEORGE

SINGLE MALT

WHISKEY

ST. GEORGE SINGLE MALT WHISKEY

When master distiller Lance Winters began working at the Bay Area's St. George Spirits in 1996, one of the first things he did was make a single malt whiskey. He created the liquor's label with famed local graphic designer and artist David Lance Goines, who had previously dreamed up Ravenswood Winery's iconic logo.

CORK & BOTTLE PRIVATE STOCK KENTUCKY STRAIGHT BOURBON WHISKEY

In 1970, Cork & Bottle, a liquor store on New York's Upper East Side, which is still open today, offered its own four-year-old bourbon made by Jim Beam.

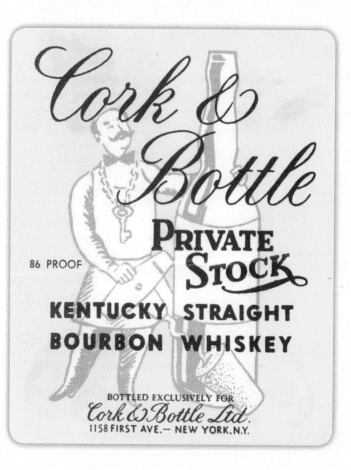

BEAM'S CHOICE

Groovy Braniff International Airways (which went out of business in 1982) not only offered alcohol on its flights, but it also served minis of its own special (and equally hip) eight-year-old Beam's Choice. Not to be outdone, Continental Air Lines stocked its own version of Beam's Choice.

BEAM'S PRIVATE STOCK KENTUCKY STRAIGHT BOURBON WHISKEY

In the early 1970s, diners at Kung Pei Cocktail Lounge in Albuquerque, New Mexico, could order a special 86-proof, four-year-old Jim Beam bourbon. The overall label and the bar's logo make for an interesting mix of traditional and faux-Asian design.

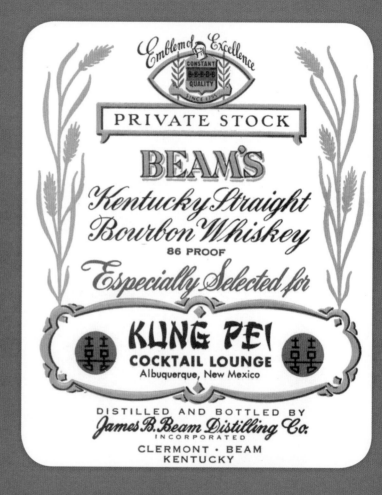

Emblem of Excellence

CONSTANT B·B·B·B QUALITY

SINCE 1795

PRIVATE STOCK

BEAM'S

Kentucky Straight Bourbon Whiskey

86 PROOF

Especially Selected for

KUNG PEI
COCKTAIL LOUNGE
Albuquerque, New Mexico

DISTILLED AND BOTTLED BY
James B. Beam Distilling Co.
INCORPORATED

CLERMONT · BEAM
KENTUCKY

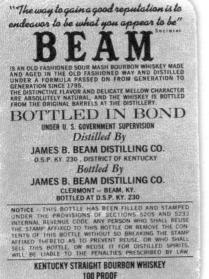

BONDED BEAM KENTUCKY STRAIGHT BOURBON WHISKEY

Jim Beam was going for the top shelf with this 1976 oval label for its eight-year-old, 100-proof bonded bourbon. The corresponding label on the back of the bottle even featured a quote from Socrates: "The way to gain a good reputation is to endeavor to be what you appear to be."

COLONEL JAMES B. BEAM
KENTUCKY STRAIGHT
BOURBON WHISKEY

This old-timey label was used in the 1970s and honors Jim Beam's namesake, who restarted the company after Prohibition and laid the foundation for the brand's success.

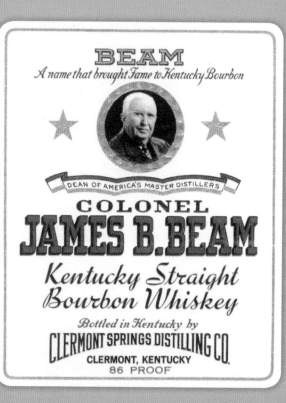

J. W. DANT
SPECIAL RESERVE KENTUCKY STRAIGHT BOURBON WHISKEY

While this label dates to the 1970s, it looks much older and was no doubt an attempt to appeal to drinkers' sense of nostalgia and to give the affordable spirit a bit of class.

MARION CORN
CORN WHISKEY

At 100 proof and under a
month old, this white whiskey
was not for the faint of heart.
But the label is surprisingly
elegant.

PROOF **100** PROOF

MARION CORN

CORN

WHISKEY

Bottled by
The Clear Spring Distilling Co.

Clermont, Kentucky

OLD TUB
KENTUCKY STRAIGHT
BOURBON WHISKEY

Before Prohibition, Jim Beam's bourbon was known as Old Tub. Though this pint label looks like it dates from the late 1800s, it was actually used in 1977. The back of the bottle said: "An old fashioned bourbon whiskey made and aged in the old fashioned way."

CHICAGO YACHT CLUB JAMES B. BEAM
KENTUCKY STRAIGHT BOURBON WHISKEY

Like many private clubs, the Chicago Yacht Club boasted its own special bottling of Jim Beam bourbon. The label features beautiful boat renderings and the club's official flag, which it still uses today.

GEORGE DICKEL TENNESSEE SOUR MASH WHISKY MERLE HAGGARD JUG

To honor its long-serving brand ambassador, country music legend Merle Haggard, Dickel sold this jug filled with Tennessee whiskey in the 1970s and early 1980s with his portrait on the back and the quote "Ain't Nothin' Better."

GEORGE DICKEL TENNESSEE SOUR MASH WHISKY POWDER HORNS

George Dickel sold its whiskey in so-called decorative powder horns for years. This pair dates from the 1970s—a perfect match for the fringed fashions of the day.

WILD TURKEY LIQUEUR WITH HONEY

In the 1970s Wild Turkey tried to sweeten up its image—and appeal to female drinkers—with a bourbon-based honey liqueur. The spirit was a departure from its whiskey, and the decanter-like bottle was quite different from that of its famous 101 bourbon.

COCKTAILS OF THE TIME

From the Sex on the Beach and the Alabama Slammer to the Harvey Wallbanger, cocktails of the 1970s, 1980s, and 1990s weren't known for subtlety (or quality). In many places, style trumped quality (think Tom Cruise throwing bottles around in the late-1980s film *Cocktail*). Drinkers were also discovering and developing a love for vodka, sales of which went through the roof during this period. The sudden ascendancy of the spirit came at whiskey's expense—its sales declined rapidly. Those who did order bourbon, rye, or Tennessee whiskies often mixed them with beer or even Coca-Cola. Desperate times called for desperate measures.

While Whiskey and Cokes and Boilermakers are still popular—especially with college students—I would suggest fixing talented bartender and cocktail consultant Aisha Sharpe's Beggar's Banquet, a modern sophisticated twist on the era's drinks. Her concoction, which she created for the drinks menu at the Breslin restaurant inside New York's hip Ace Hotel, calls for both bourbon and beer, as well as some fresh lemon juice and a bit of sweet maple syrup.

BOILERMAKER

12 ounces beer
1½ ounces whiskey
GLASS: Pint and shot glass

»»» Pour the beer into a pint glass. Pour the whiskey into a shot glass and drop it—glass and all—into the beer.

BEGGAR'S BANQUET

CONTRIBUTED BY AISHA SHARPE

2 dashes Fee Brothers Whiskey Barrel–Aged Bitters
¼ ounce fresh lemon juice
¾ ounce maple syrup
2 ounces Maker's Mark Bourbon
Old Speckled Hen Beer
GARNISH: ½ orange wheel
GLASS: Highball

»»» Put all the ingredients except the beer in a shaker and fill with ice. Shake and then strain into a highball glass filled with fresh ice. Top with beer and garnish with the orange.

DISTILLING LEGEND
FREDERICK BOOKER NOE II

Frederick Booker Noe II didn't set out to revolutionize the world, but he did just that by introducing his Small Batch Bourbon Collection in 1992.

More than forty years earlier, as a student at the University of Kentucky, Booker played football for Hall of Fame coach Bear Bryant before dropping out. He soon joined the family business, Jim Beam Bourbon; his grandfather was none other than distiller Jim Beam.

Being related to Jim Beam himself, however, didn't mean a cushy desk job. For one, there were plenty of other Beams employed at the distillery, and the family was still trying to get the operation up and running after shutting down for Prohibition and the disruption of World War II.

By all accounts, Booker distinguished himself as a hard worker and learned how to make whiskey from his cousin, Carl Beam, and his great-uncle, T. Jeremiah Beam. To keep up with demand for its famous white label bourbon, Bonded Beam, and Beam's Choice, the company bought a second facility, the Churchill Downs Distillery in Boston, Kentucky, in 1954, and put Booker in charge in 1960.

While these days a master distiller is expected to create new and interesting spirits every year, up until recently most brands had only a few core bottlings that never changed. Booker, however, was never satisfied, always trying to refine the company's recipes and increase yields from each bushel of grain. The privacy of Boston, Kentucky, allowed him to start "playing with the stuff on his own," says Fred Booker Noe III, his son and the brand's seventh-generation master distiller. "He was looking for something different."

Beginning in the late 1970s, Booker began experimenting, distilling the whiskey at different proofs, varying the positions of the casks in the warehouses, and blending small batches of particularly delicious bourbons. (He wasn't alone: in 1984 his good friend, Elmer T. Lee, master distiller at George T. Stagg, released the world's first single barrel bourbon, called Blanton's Single Barrel.)

Slowly word got out that Booker had created something delicious. It couldn't have come at a better time. After decades of robust sales, the company and the overall whiskey industry were losing market share to beer, wine, and, unbelievably, vodka and single malt Scotch (both upstarts at the time). Beam's corporate office in Chicago persuaded him to share his new uncut barrel-strength whiskey and convinced him to name it Booker's. To test the market for a small-batch bourbon,

they sent bottles of it to their distributors around the country as a Christmas gift. Booker handwrote the label. He chose a wine-like bottle, dipped the top in brown wax, and packed it in a wooden box—packaging that remains the same today.

"The response was overwhelming," says Fred Noe. "As they say, history was made." Booker's popularity—arguably the first small-batch and the first successful super-premium bourbon—led to the creation of Beam's Small Batch Bourbon Collection, which includes Basil Hayden's, Baker's, and Knob Creek. All the whiskies were unique, made with different recipes and aged for various amounts of time. They offered bigger and more interesting flavor profiles and were packed in a range of unconventional and interesting bottles, which appealed to a younger generation.

Baker's also comes in a wine-like bottle but is dipped in black wax and affixed with a label that looks block-printed. Knob Creek's bottle resembles a square pharmaceutical pint

with a modern, font-heavy approach. Basil Hayden's features a long, wide parchment label that fits the bottle like a tunic and is belted with a wood-and-metal band.

Booker passed away in 2004. The bourbons he created ushered in a new era of American whiskey making and connoisseurship, not to mention a new era of package design. "Booker," says Fred Noe, "was a step ahead."

◄—« **Booker Noe and his dog are immortalized in this bronze statue on the grounds of the Jim Beam distillery.**

7

The NEW GOLDEN AGE

The Bourbon in this bottle is one of the first [*legal*] whiskeys to be produced in the New York State since Prohibition. Made from New York State [*corn*], double-distilled and aged in a small charred [*oak*] cask. Our Baby Bourbon owes its [*rich*] [*color and*] character to the small barrel aging process [*used by our*] distiller. A uniquely warm spirit, suitable [*for any*] occasion. We are very happy to share it [*with you.*] Baby Bourbon is the first bourbon distilled [*and*] produced at the Tuthilltown Gristmill, a National [*landmark.*]

Year ___07___   Batch ___13___

It's certainly a great time to be an American whiskey drinker. There is an amazing selection of bourbon, rye, Tennessee, and even unaged whiskies made by both large famous brands and small upstarts across the country.

No matter the size of the operation, distillers are embracing exotic ingredients (care for a dram of sorghum-based whiskey?) and innovative techniques like smoking the grain before it's distilled.

In fact, the industry can no longer keep up with international demand and is rapidly expanding distilleries and building new warehouses. In 2012, more than one million barrels of bourbon were filled. It was the first time since 1973, according to the Kentucky Distillers Association, that the number of barrels produced reached seven digits. For the last several years, there have been more bourbon barrels aging than people in the entire state of Kentucky. And in 2013, according to DISCUS,

PREVIOUS PAGE: Chip Tate is making some of today's most acclaimed and interesting whiskies at his distillery Balcones, in Waco, Texas.

◀—◀◀ Labeling day for Hudson Baby Bourbon at Tuthilltown Spirits' distillery in New York's Hudson Valley. It was the state's first (legal) whiskey producer to open after Prohibition ended.

bourbon and Tennessee whiskey set a new record with exports totaling more than $1 billion.

Former niche whiskey Maker's Mark, which not that long ago sold most of its bottles in its home state of Kentucky, now sells more than one million nine-liter cases every year around the world. And you can forget about getting yourself some Pappy Van Winkle, which is arguably the hottest spirit in the country. Supplies are so tight that even the best liquor stores only get a couple of bottles each year. (Read more about who Pappy Van Winkle actually was and his family later in this chapter, starting on page 173.)

What spurred this new golden age of distilling? The short answer is the birth of small-batch whiskies that challenged the supremacy of single malt Scotches and garnered respect from connoisseurs and bartenders alike. The rebirth of the cocktail also helped to get Americans drinking domestic whiskies again. Mustachioed, suspender-wearing mixologists in faux speakeasies became immediate fans of these high-proof and well-made whiskies, which are required to fix many classic pre-Prohibition tipples that are currently in vogue.

At the same time, many people have gotten a lot savvier about food and drink in general and are interested in not only consuming the final product but also hearing the story behind it. This sudden curiosity has made a number of distillers practically celebrities, and they now spend their time traveling the world leading tastings, shaking hands, and signing bottles. The liquor brands have also taken notice of this movement and emphasize the craftsmanship and artisanal nature of their products—no matter how many cases they sell a year.

Designer Spirits

The golden age doesn't stop with distilling. With all the competition on store shelves and on the back bar, American whiskey brands have created an array of labels that run the gamut from charmingly retro to thoroughly modern. Package design is king.

Some of these labels, like Barterhouse and Few, hearken back to the early 1900s with old-timey lettering and vintage-looking logos, while others, like Balcones and Angel's Envy, have embraced new fonts, graphics, and bottle shapes.

So pour yourself a few fingers of your favorite dram and toast this whiskey boom!

COLONEL E. H. TAYLOR SINGLE BARREL STRAIGHT KENTUCKY BOURBON WHISKEY

In 2011, when Buffalo Trace reintroduced this brand that was originally available in the early 1900s, it had trouble tracking down a copy of the original label. Fortunately, one of the Colonel's descendants had a bottle in his attic.

PAPPY VAN WINKLE'S FAMILY RESERVE 15 YEARS OLD KENTUCKY STRAIGHT BOURBON WHISKEY

This is one of the hardest bottles to get your hands on no matter how much money you're willing to spend. Ironically, the Pappy Van Winkle Family Reserve line was created because the brand wasn't able to sell its younger whiskey, leaving it with a surplus of mature bourbon after a few years.

OLD RIP VAN WINKLE HANDMADE BOURBON AGED 10 YEARS

While the Pappy Van Winkle's Family Reserve series is extremely popular with drinkers and collectors, a bottle of the younger Old Rip Van Winkle shouldn't be ignored. Even though the label looks practically antediluvian, the brand only dates back to the 1970s.

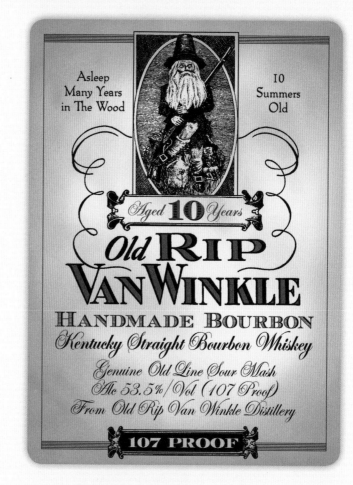

Asleep Many Years in The Wood

10 Summers Old

Aged **10** *Years*

Old **RIP**

VanWinkle

HANDMADE BOURBON

Kentucky Straight Bourbon Whiskey

Genuine Old Line Sour Mash

Alc 53.5%/Vol (107 Proof)

From Old Rip Van Winkle Distillery

107 PROOF

MAKER'S MARK KENTUCKY STRAIGHT BOURBON WHISKY

Since its first bottle of bourbon was dipped in red wax in 1958, the homespun packaging for Maker's Mark hasn't changed much and remains easy to recognize.

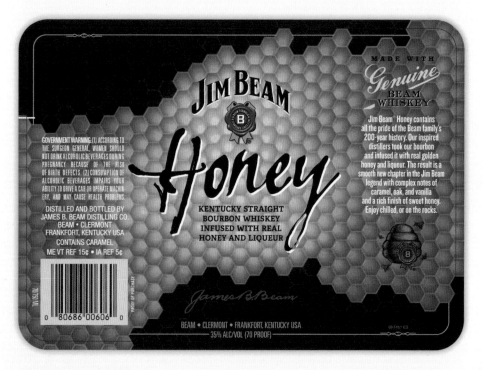

MADE WITH
Genuine
BEAM
WHISKEY

Jim Beam® Honey contains all the pride of the Beam family's 200-year history. Our inspired distillers took our bourbon and infused it with real golden honey and liqueur. The result is a smooth new chapter in the Jim Beam legend with complex notes of caramel, oak, and vanilla and a rich finish of sweet honey. Enjoy chilled, or on the rocks.

JIM BEAM

Honey

KENTUCKY STRAIGHT
BOURBON WHISKEY
INFUSED WITH REAL
HONEY AND LIQUEUR

GOVERNMENT WARNING: (1) ACCORDING TO THE SURGEON GENERAL, WOMEN SHOULD NOT DRINK ALCOHOLIC BEVERAGES DURING PREGNANCY, BECAUSE OF THE RISK OF BIRTH DEFECTS. (2) CONSUMPTION OF ALCOHOLIC BEVERAGES IMPAIRS YOUR ABILITY TO DRIVE A CAR OR OPERATE MACHINERY, AND MAY CAUSE HEALTH PROBLEMS.

DISTILLED AND BOTTLED BY JAMES B. BEAM DISTILLING CO.
BEAM • CLERMONT
FRANKFORT, KENTUCKY USA
CONTAINS CARAMEL
ME VT REF 15¢ • IA REF 5¢

0 80686 00606 0

James B Beam

BEAM • CLERMONT • FRANKFORT, KENTUCKY USA
35% ALC/VOL (70 PROOF)

JIM BEAM HONEY

Thanks to honey liqueurs like Wild Turkey American Honey, sweet bourbon-based liqueurs have exploded, with drinkers around the country ordering these spirits. Jim Beam Honey, which came out in 2013 after first launching in Germany, features an eye-catching honeycomb label that includes a small beehive.

ST. GEORGE SINGLE MALT WHISKEY

In 2011, acclaimed St. George Spirits began using a new shorter and wider bottle for its single malt whiskey. The Bay Area brand also updated the spirit's label, which still features its signature fire-breathing dragon but now has an old-world feel similar to an engraved stock certificate.

ST. GEORGE SINGLE MALT WHISKEY 30TH ANNIVERSARY EDITION

Jörg Rupf is one of the fathers of the craft-distilling movement in America, having founded St. George Spirits back in 1982. To honor the brand's thirtieth anniversary, the distillers released just 715 bottles of a special edition of its single malt whiskey that includes a mix of old and rare spirits finished in a barrel that held its pear eau-de-vie.

SINGLE
BARREL
SOUR MASH

Elmer T. Lee

KENTUCKY
STRAIGHT
BOURBON
WHISKEY

45% ALC BY VOL
(90 PROOF)

ELMER T. LEE SINGLE BARREL KENTUCKY STRAIGHT BOURBON WHISKEY

Every bourbon drinker should know the name Elmer T. Lee. He created the world's first single barrel bourbon, Blanton's, when he was the master distiller at George T. Stagg. In honor of his retirement in 1986, the distillery introduced Elmer T. Lee Single Barrel, for which Lee helped select the casks until he died in 2013.

FOUR ROSES SINGLE BARREL
KENTUCKY STRAIGHT BOURBON WHISKEY

For many years, the only way to buy Four Roses Bourbon was to get on a plane, since the nonblended version of the whiskey was only available in foreign markets. Fortunately, the bourbon, including its Single Barrel, which comes in an impressive, statuesque bottle, is now back on store shelves.

ANGEL'S ENVY CASK STRENGTH
KENTUCKY STRAIGHT BOURBON WHISKEY

Master distiller and Bourbon Hall of Fame member Lincoln Henderson's final project before he passed away was creating this small-batch whiskey. For this bottling, he picked the barrels, blended the whiskey, and finished the spirit in used port casks.

MAKER'S 46
KENTUCKY BOURBON WHISKY

After decades of making just one product, Maker's Mark introduced 46 in 2010. It is created by aging regular Maker's a second time in special barrels; the bottle is an updated version of the standard square Maker's container and, of course, is still covered in dripping red wax.

OLD BLOWHARD
KENTUCKY BOURBON WHISKEY

No one would blame you for thinking that Old Blowhard is a historic brand, but it debuted in 2014. The twenty-six-year-old bourbon is part of international spirits conglomerate Diageo's Orphan Barrel Whiskey Distilling Co. project, which bottles extremely rare and limited-edition spirits.

BARTERHOUSE KENTUCKY BOURBON

This fanciful label belongs to a twenty-year-old bourbon that was aging in an old Stitzel-Weller warehouse in Louisville and is also part of Diageo's Orphan Barrel project.

BOOKER'S BOURBON
BATCH NO. 2014-01

Booker's Bourbon helped start an international frenzy for American whiskey. To honor the twenty-fifth anniversary of this landmark liquor's release, and its creator Booker Noe, Jim Beam created a limited edition of the spirit. The label includes text from the original label and an image of Booker's famous rocking chair.

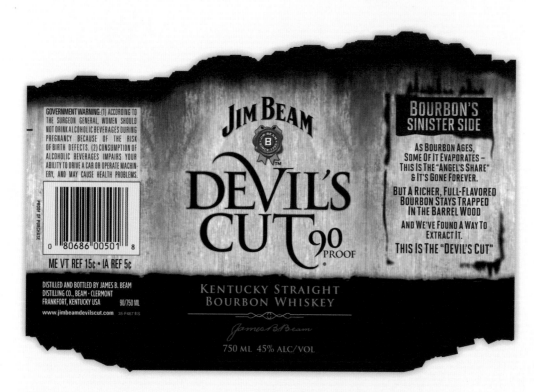

GOVERNMENT WARNING: (1) ACCORDING TO THE SURGEON GENERAL, WOMEN SHOULD NOT DRINK ALCOHOLIC BEVERAGES DURING PREGNANCY BECAUSE OF THE RISK OF BIRTH DEFECTS. (2) CONSUMPTION OF ALCOHOLIC BEVERAGES IMPAIRS YOUR ABILITY TO DRIVE A CAR OR OPERATE MACHINERY, AND MAY CAUSE HEALTH PROBLEMS.

PROOF OF PURCHASE

0 80686 00501 8

ME VT REF 15¢ • IA REF 5¢

DISTILLED AND BOTTLED BY JAMES B. BEAM DISTILLING CO., BEAM • CLERMONT FRANKFORT, KENTUCKY USA
www.jimbeamdevilscut.com   35-F467 ES   90/750 ML

JIM BEAM

B
SINCE 1795

™

DEVIL'S CUT 90 PROOF

KENTUCKY STRAIGHT BOURBON WHISKEY

James B. Beam

750 ML   45% ALC/VOL

BOURBON'S SINISTER SIDE

AS BOURBON AGES, SOME OF IT EVAPORATES – THIS IS THE "ANGEL'S SHARE" & IT'S GONE FOREVER.

BUT A RICHER, FULL-FLAVORED BOURBON STAYS TRAPPED IN THE BARREL WOOD

AND WE'VE FOUND A WAY TO EXTRACT IT.

THIS IS THE "DEVIL'S CUT"

JIM BEAM DEVIL'S CUT KENTUCKY STRAIGHT BOURBON WHISKEY

Barrels unfailingly soak up some of the whiskey they hold, which is called the devil's cut. Jim Beam has developed a system, similar to a giant paint shaker, that gets the barrels to give back this oaky and tannic whiskey, which is then mixed with Beam's regular bourbon to create its Devil's Cut.

WILD TURKEY AMERICAN HONEY

When Wild Turkey relaunched its bourbon-based honey liqueur in 2006—thirty years after it was originally introduced—it set off a craze for flavored whiskies, which is still going strong.

HILLROCK ESTATE DISTILLERY
SINGLE MALT WHISKEY

This is one bottle you'll want to display prominently in your home. The impressive (and hefty) decanter showcases the Hudson Valley brand's logo in gold and has an intricate side label and a wooden stopper. The whiskey is also quite delicious: no surprise, since former Maker's Mark master distiller Dave Pickerell oversees Hillrock Estate.

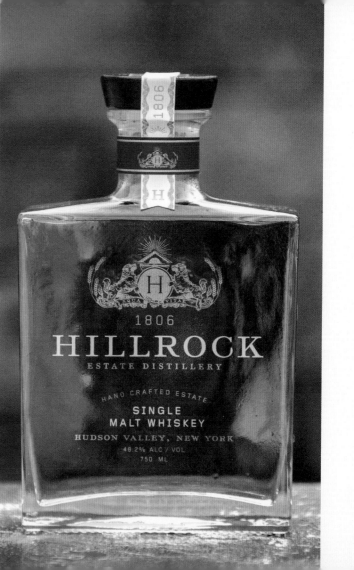

KOVAL SINGLE BARREL MILLET WHISKEY

Koval was the first distillery to open in Chicago after Prohibition ended and has won acclaim for its line of whiskies made from a range of organic grains. Its bottles are like sleek modern versions of apothecary jars with appropriately modern and spare labels.

FEW BOURBON WHISKEY

Evanston, Illinois, was, remarkably, completely dry until the 1970s but now boasts a craft distillery. Few's bourbon label evokes the 1893 Chicago World's Fair and includes a statue built for the event that stood almost half as tall as New York's Statue of Liberty.

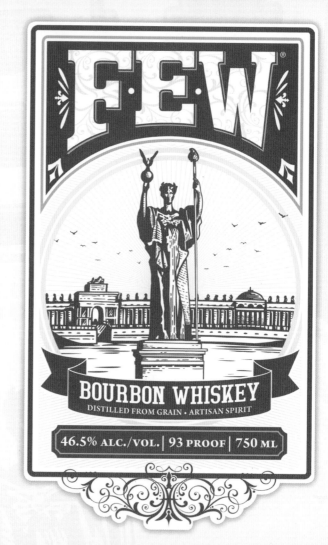

45.2% ALC/VOL (90.4 PROOF) 750 ML

RAGTIME RYE
AMERICAN STRAIGHT WHISKEY

Put on some Scott Joplin and pour yourself a slug of this rye whiskey from the New York Distilling Company. The brand's detailed label looks like it could be a still from a graphic novel about the era's piano players.

WILLETT POT STILL RESERVE KENTUCKY STRAIGHT BOURBON WHISKEY

For its Pot Still Reserve bourbon, Willett
was inspired by its still. The elegant glass
bottle is shaped like the distillery's copper
pot still and is so unique it can be easily
spotted from across a bar.

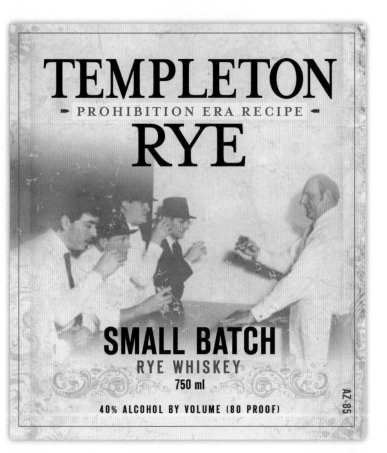

TEMPLETON
- PROHIBITION ERA RECIPE -
RYE

SMALL BATCH
RYE WHISKEY
750 ml
40% ALCOHOL BY VOLUME (80 PROOF)

AZ-85

TEMPLETON SMALL BATCH RYE WHISKEY

According to legend, notorious gangster and bootlegger Al Capone was partial to the whiskey produced in Templeton, Iowa. This bit of history inspired the founders of this local distillery and is reflected in its vintage-looking label.

HUDSON SINGLE MALT WHISKEY

The Hudson Valley's Tuthilltown Spirits was a trailblazer when it opened in 2005. It was the state's first whiskey distillery after Prohibition ended and helped kick-start the craft distilling movement. Its signature line of Hudson whiskies, which was sold to William Grant & Sons in 2010, is packed in distinctive glass bottles.

NOAH'S MILL
BOURBON WHISKEY

This potent whiskey—a stiff 114.3 proof—comes in a simple bottle with a single-color label that looks like it dates back to frontier times.

BALCONES BABY BLUE CORN WHISKY

One of the top new American whiskies is made in, of all places, Waco, Texas. And Balcones Baby Blue Corn Whisky is actually produced completely from roasted blue cornmeal. Its thoroughly modern label emphasizes the liquor's main ingredient by featuring a corn stalk.

BALCONES BRIMSTONE TEXAS SCRUB OAK SMOKED CORN WHISKY

With a striking name like Brimstone, you have to bring the fire and drama. Balcones certainly delivers with this corn whiskey that is smoked with local Texas scrub oak. The label reflects its origins with an Old West–style font (think *Tombstone*) and features a shock of bright red flame.

MICHTER'S 10 YEARS OLD SINGLE BARREL STRAIGHT RYE WHISKEY

Talk about a legacy: according to lore, George Washington bought Michter's rye for his Revolutionary War troops. The brand, which was founded in Pennsylvania, went out of business in the 1980s but was resurrected in the 1990s and is now based in Kentucky.

CORSAIR
SINGLE BARREL
TRIPLE SMOKE

AMERICAN MALT WHISKEY
POT DISTILLED FROM
CHERRY, BEECHWOOD, AND PEAT SMOKED BARLEY
50% ALC/VOL (100 PROOF)

CORSAIR TRIPLE SMOKE SINGLE BARREL AMERICAN MALT WHISKEY

There are few spirits that can match the swagger of Corsair. All of its bottlings—including this whiskey, which is made from malted barley that has been treated with cherrywood, beechwood, and peat smoke—feature a highly stylized image of its founders.

LARCENY KENTUCKY STRAIGHT BOURBON WHISKEY

You won't break the law by drinking this wheated Kentucky bourbon. The origins of the catchy name come from a legend about a thieving treasury agent who stole whiskey samples from the warehouse he was supposed to be guarding.

**WHIPPERSNAPPER
OREGON SPIRIT WHISKEY**

This beautiful label adorns Ransom Spirits' American whiskey, which is made in a traditional pot still, using the most traditional of techniques. For drinkers who are interested, the story of the whiskey is right on the bottle.

TINCUP AMERICAN WHISKEY

Tincup isn't just a cute name: the American whiskey actually comes with a small metal cup on top of its hexagonal glass bottle and is an homage to the drinking vessels miners used in Colorado. While the label is relatively small, the packaging is certainly attention grabbing.

HENRY DUYORE'S STRAIGHT BOURBON WHISKEY

While this straight bourbon whiskey may be made in Sheridan, Oregon, its roots lie with illicit distillers making moonshine in Virginia's backwoods. The image is of a real moonshiner working in the wilds of Appalachia.

HIGH WEST
SON OF BOURYE WHISKEY

Love both bourbon and rye whiskey? Then you need to try this unusual blend that mixes the two spirits. The label plays up this Frankensteinian concept with an illustration of a pair of mythical jackalopes.

ESTABLISHED 1993

OLD POTRERO®

TRADITIONAL · ANCHOR DISTILLING CO. · POT DISTILLED
A
TRADEMARK
SAN FRANCISCO

SINGLE MALT
STRAIGHT RYE
WHISKEY

*Pot distilled and aged in
new charred oak barrels*

DISTILLED, AGED AND BOTTLED BY
ANCHOR DISTILLING COMPANY
SAN FRANCISCO, CALIFORNIA

750 ml

48.5% Alc/vol
(97 Proof)

OLD POTRERO SINGLE MALT STRAIGHT RYE WHISKEY

Fritz Maytag helped start the craft-beer renaissance in the United States, and in 1996 he tackled a similarly difficult task: getting Americans to drink rye whiskey. Not only was he committed to making the spirit with a traditional pot still and from historic recipes, but he also used an old-timey bell-shaped bottle with throwback labels, which over the years haven't changed much.

KINGS COUNTY DISTILLERY
CHOCOLATE "FLAVORED" WHISKEY

What happens when you soak cacao bean husks, which have been used to make artisanal Mast Brothers Chocolate, in unaged corn whiskey? Brooklyn's Kings County didn't know until it tried making this delicious spirit a few years ago. The distillery uses its standard bottle and label for the chocolate "flavored" whiskey, which gives the liquor a sleek, lab-like feel.

KINGS COUNTY DISTILLERY
chocolate "flavored" whiskey
40% alcohol by volume, 200ml

STRANAHAN'S COLORADO WHISKEY

Colorado may be famous for its beer breweries, but Stranahan's is trying to change the state's reputation with its Colorado Whiskey. The statuesque bottle is draped with an eye-catching yellow-and-black label that features both the Rockies and the elevation of the distillery—5,280 feet—and is capped with a reusable metal jigger.

COCKTAILS OF THE TIME

While you can still find plenty of joints serving classics like Old-Fashioneds, Manhattans, and Mint Juleps, bartenders across the country are creating innovative recipes that call for a range of American whiskies.

Here are three concoctions from Larry Rice, the owner of top Louisville bar Silver Dollar. The Spaghetti Western combines bourbon with the Italian aperitif Aperol, the Dry Wit mixes whiskey with dry vermouth, and the Honky Tonk calls for Rittenhouse Rye and Spanish Cardenal Mendoza Brandy, which adds a maple note.

DRY WIT

CONTRIBUTED BY LARRY RICE

2 ounces W.L. Weller Special Reserve Bourbon

1 ounce dry vermouth (preferably Dolin Dry or Vya Extra Dry)

3 dashes Angostura Bitters

3 dashes Regans' Orange Bitters No. 6

¼ ounce Demerara syrup (a mix of two parts Demerara sugar and one part water)

GARNISH: Orange peel

GLASS: Cocktail

⟫⟫ Put all the ingredients in a mixing glass and fill with ice. Stir and then strain into a chilled cocktail glass. Twist the orange peel over the glass to express its oils and then discard the peel.

SPAGHETTI WESTERN

CONTRIBUTED BY LARRY RICE

2 ounces Four Roses Single Barrel Bourbon

1 ounce fresh lime juice

1 ounce simple syrup (a mix of equal parts sugar and water)

½ ounce Aperol

1 egg white

GARNISH: 3 dashes Angostura Bitters

GLASS: Cocktail

⟫⟫ Put all the ingredients in a shaker and fill with ice. Shake vigorously and then strain into a cocktail glass. Garnish the top of the drink with the bitters.

HONKY TONK

CONTRIBUTED BY LARRY RICE

¼ ounce Green Chartreuse

2 ounces Rittenhouse Rye

½ ounce Cardenal Mendoza Spanish Brandy

⅛ ounce Demerara syrup (a mix of two parts Demerara sugar and one part water)

3 dashes Scrappy's Rootbeer Bitters

3 dashes Angostura Bitters

GARNISH: Orange peel

GLASS: Cocktail

⟫⟫ Rinse a cocktail glass with the Green Chartreuse and pour off any excess. Put the rest of the ingredients in a mixing glass and fill with ice. Stir and then strain into the rinsed glass. Twist the orange peel over the glass to express its oils, then discard the peel.

DISTILLING LEGEND
JULIAN P. "PAPPY" VAN WINKLE

Forget about bottles of first-growth Bordeaux wine from 1982—the holy grail for drinkers these days is Pappy Van Winkle bourbon. (I'm not even going to mention the brand's rye, which is also virtually impossible to find.)

The favorite of whiskey aficionados, bartenders, and chefs is a sensation with ample media coverage, including a giant feature in the *Wall Street Journal* detailing the lengths to which people will go to procure a taste of the rare dram. When several cases of the whiskey were stolen from a warehouse in 2013, the crime was national news and a $10,000 reward for tips leading to an arrest was offered.

But the story behind the brand and its popular whiskies is arguably even more interesting than what's inside the bottle. For starters, Pappy Van Winkle was a real person and not the creation of a marketing firm.

In 1893, Julian P. "Pappy" Van Winkle Sr. began working as a traveling salesman for Louisville-based wholesaler W. L. Weller & Sons. He covered northern Kentucky and journeyed from Louisville to Cincinnati by horse and buggy selling bourbons produced by the local A. Ph. Stitzel Distillery, and other spirits, to bars. "He pretty much stayed out on the road for weeks," says his grandson Julian Van Winkle III.

Before Prohibition, Pappy and his partner, Alex Farnsley, bought both W. L. Weller and the Stitzel Distillery, eventually combining them to create the Stitzel-Weller Distillery. (It was one of the lucky few to be allowed to sell medicinal whiskey during the famously dry period.) The new company built up a robust portfolio of whiskies, including W. L. Weller, Old Fitzgerald, and Cabin Still. (You can find all three on store shelves today.)

Pappy wasn't shy about making whiskey. A sign on his distillery's gate read, "We make fine bourbon . . . at a profit if we can . . . at a loss if we must . . . *but always fine bourbon.*"

He also ran a series of advertorials in national magazines, including *Time* and *Sports Illustrated.* One published in 1954 was titled "What Is Your Whiskey IQ," in which he cleared up a number of common myths he often encountered, including the claim that whiskey starts off with a red hue. (For the record, it's clear when it comes off the still. The barrel gives the spirit all of its color.) "He caught the public eye," says his grandson. Pappy ran the Stitzel-Weller company until late 1964 and passed away just a few months later, in February of 1965, at the age of ninety.

Like the rest of the bourbon industry, the Van Winkles found themselves in a tough position in 1972. "The business wasn't great," admits Van Winkle III. Their stockholders insisted that the company be sold to conglomerate Norton Simon Inc.

However, Pappy's son, Julian Van Winkle Jr., was able to retain one special holding: the Old Rip Van Winkle line. It wasn't much more than a name, since the brand hadn't been used in decades. And Van Winkle Jr. didn't have a distillery or a warehouse full of liquor.

But he was able to buy some seven-year-old whiskey back from Norton Simon, since at the time it and the other big whiskey brands had plenty of barrels to sell. "He was lucky enough to have aged whiskey right off the bat," says his son. "Just impossible to do today."

Without a distillery and its marquee whiskies, how could the company survive? Well, with a lot of hard work and some luck. Over the years, Van Winkle Jr. continued to source delicious whiskies from a range of bigger brands and word began to slowly spread. He passed away in 1981 and his son, Julian Van Winkle III, took over the business.

Throughout the rest of the decade the decorative-decanter market helped keep the company afloat. It wasn't until the late 1990s that Van Winkle III dreamed up the revered Family Reserve line of bourbon. By chance he came across a black-and-white, 8½ x 11-inch glossy photo of his grandfather smoking a cigar, and it triggered an idea to create a special whiskey. "I designed it around that photo," he remembers. "It was real organic." With the help of a local artist he turned the image into a label and chose a stock cognac bottle that he'd been using for other spirits.

Not only was it a chance to honor his grandfather, but it also solved another problem: Van Winkle III was sitting on a stock of excess mature whiskey that he didn't know what to do with. At the time people weren't hounding him (or other distillers for that matter) night and day for twenty-year-old whiskies.

But buying whiskey on the open market was getting progressively harder as drinkers began to develop a thirst for bourbon and rye. In 2002, Van Winkle III solved his supply troubles by finding a permanent home for his whiskies. Buffalo Trace, which in addition to its eponymous brand owns Sazerac Rye, Blanton's, W. L. Weller (yes, Pappy's original bourbon), and a number of other delicious American whiskies, agreed to produce the full line of Van Winkle's products.

The most sought-after Pappy Van Winkle's Family (Reserve 15 Years Old, 20 Years Old, and 23 Years Old) continue to be released in small allotments, which are snapped up almost immediately. These bottlings contain spirits Van Winkle bought from other distillers, but in the next few years all the Van Winkle whiskies will have been made at Buffalo Trace. "The new supply is working its way into our brands," he says. Fortunately, that also means there will be an increase in the amount available. (Hopefully, drinkers who have been dying to try the whiskies will find them as good as they imagined.)

If you're frustrated that you can't get your hands on a bottle, it's important to remember that forecasting supply and demand has always been tough for distillers.

Pappy even addressed the problem in an advertorial, titled *How to Get a Full Night's Sleep*, that ran in an October 1957 issue of the *New Yorker*.

"One peculiarity of our business is that production is always four to eight years ahead of our market. Which might worry some folks! Since there's no way of guessing what's around the corner that far ahead, we operate on the principle that there will always be enough customers who appreciate our kind of whiskey to use up the limited amount we're able to make at the price we've got to ask. So we pay no mind to the long-haired prognosticators, get our full night's sleep, and keep our still abubbling!"

I'll drink to that!

»» ACKNOWLEDGMENTS ««

The origin of this book starts with a very early flight I took to Louisville, Kentucky, several years ago.

I was traveling down to meet Bill Samuels Jr. and get a sneak peek at his new Maker's 46 bourbon. Samuels had agreed to pick me up and drive me to the Maker's Mark Distillery, since the airport wasn't too far out of his way. Along the ride, he decided that we should take some detours. Who was I to argue?

One of the stops was at Heaven Hill's fine Bourbon Heritage Center. As I wandered the galleries, I was struck by a display of historic whiskey labels and bottles. Almost immediately I realized that this artwork would be the perfect subject for a book. But it took several years and the help of dozens of people to make that idea into a reality.

This book wouldn't have happened without the unending support, love, and patience of my smart (and grammatically inclined) wife, Ingrid. My parents and sister were excited from the start about the project, and their encouragement means the world to me.

I need to thank my agent Farley Chase for helping to shape the book proposal and getting Ten Speed Press on board. My extremely talented editor Emily Timberlake got me and this project from the first time we talked; a writer couldn't ask for a better working relationship. The design Betsy Stromberg created elegantly showcases the beauty and artistry that these labels so deserve.

My gratitude to Michael R. Veach, who is a fount of knowledge about all things bourbon. Same goes for David Wondrich, who is the definitive source for historical cocktail knowledge. I am grateful that Dale DeGroff, Allen Katz, Gary Regan, Larry Rice, Jim Meehan, and Aisha Sharpe were kind enough to share some of their whiskey drink recipes with me.

Jason Horn's comments and suggestions were much appreciated and helped ensure the accuracy of this book.

I also need to thank all the brands and public relations professionals for their time, research, and willingness to search for labels, images, and other obscure information, including Amanda Hathaway, Aaron Brost, Chip Tate, Winston Edwards, Andrea Duvall, Elizabeth Bingham, Amy Preske, Darek Bell, Cheetah Wayne, Mackenzie O'Brien, Paul Hletko, Dawn Bonner, Josh Hafer, Larry Kass, Kelly Hubbuch, Christa Graff, Danielle Eddy, Dan Cohen, Sonat Birnecker Hart, Jacqueline Long, Kate Kenny, Lisa Frost, Zack Nobinger, Sari Brecher, Jaclyn Sisbarro, Julian Van Winkle, Tad Seestedt, Christophe Bakunas, Ellie Winters, Laura Baddish, Sandy Levine, Hanna Lee, Gable Erenzo, Ralph Erenzo, Sarah Bessette, Andrea Braunstein, Hunter Chavanne, and the Distilled Spirits Council of the United States. Your valiant efforts were not in vain!

To all of the people who helped make this book possible and to you the reader, I raise a glass of, naturally, American whiskey. Cheers!

»» PHOTO AND ILLUSTRATION CREDITS ««

The Brown-Forman Corporation labels appear courtesy of Brown-Forman Corporation.

Willet Distillery photos copyright © 2015 by Willett Distillery.

Courtesy Ben Stechschulte: iv, 130, 133

Courtesy of Mount Vernon Ladies' Association. Photograph by Mark Gulezian: 4

Courtesy of Mount Vernon Ladies' Association. Photograph by Dan Jecha: 6

Courtesy of Mount Vernon Ladies' Association. Photograph by Russ Flint: 9

Courtesy of the Tennessee State Library and Archives, "The Saloon and Anarchy: Prohibition in Tennessee" exhibit: 9, 20

Courtesy of Brown-Forman Corporation: 12, 13, 16, 17, 18, 54, 55, 75, 76

Courtesy Buffalo Trace Distillery & the Van Winkle Family: 14, 172

Courtesy Diageo: 15, 19, 119, 120, 145, 146

Courtesy Samuels Family & Heaven Hill Distilleries: 21

Courtesy Library of Congress, Prints & Photographs Division, LC-USZ62123257: 24

Courtesy Library of Congress, Prints & Photographs Division, LC-DIG-npcc-24937: 26

Courtesy Library of Congress, Prints & Photographs Division, LC-USZ62-15182: 29

Courtesy Library of Congress, Prints & Photographs Division, LC-USZ62-95475: 29

Courtesy Library of Congress, Prints & Photographs Division, LC-USZ62-95478: 28

Courtesy Buffalo Trace Distillery & Heaven Hill Distilleries: 31

Courtesy Four Roses: 32, 46, 56, 142

Courtesy Buffalo Trace Distillery: vi, 33, 34, 35, 36, 37, 38, 39, 40, 41, 42, 43, 48, 68, 134, 135, 136, 141

Courtesy Heaven Hill Distilleries: 53, 58, 59, 62, 65, 77, 97, 115, 162

Property of the Van Winkle Family: 57, 90, 176

Courtesy Willett Distillery, photo compliments of Willett Distillery Archives: 66, 84

Courtesy David Toczko: 74

Courtesy the Samuels Family: 80

Courtesy Four Roses: 86

Courtesy Willett Distillery: 91, 92, 93, 154, 157

Courtesy Beam Suntory Inc.: 94, 95, 96, 110, 111, 112, 113, 114, 116, 117, 118, 124, 127, 137, 138, 144, 147, 148, 182

Courtesy Wild Turkey: 100, 121, 149

Courtesy Anchor Distilling: 102, 167

Courtesy Beam Suntory Inc. & the Oakland Art Novelty Company: 108

Courtesy St. George Spirits: 109, 139, 140

Courtesy Balcones: 128, 158, 159

Courtesy Angel's Envy: 143

Courtesy Hillrock Estate Distillery: 150

Courtesy Koval: Page 151

Courtesy Few: 152

Courtesy New York Distilling Company: 153

Courtesy Templeton: 155

Courtesy Tuthilltown Spirits : 156

Courtesy Michter's Distillery LLC: 160

Courtesy Corsair: 161

Courtesy Ransom Spirits & Right Arrow Key Designs: 163

Courtesy Tincup American Whiskey: 164

Courtesy Ransom Spirits (Earl Palmer photograph, Courtesy Virginia Tech Archive): 165

Courtesy High West: 166

Courtesy Kings County Distillery: 168

Courtesy Stranahan's Colorado Whiskey: 169

»» BIBLIOGRAPHY «««

Cowdery, Charles K. 2004. *Bourbon, Straight: The Uncut and Unfiltered Story of American Whiskey*. Chicago, IL: Made and Bottled in Kentucky.

Curtis, Wayne. 2006. *And a Bottle of Rum: A History of the World in Ten Cocktails*. New York: Crown.

Embury, David A. 1958. *The Fine Art of Mixing Drinks*. New York: Doubleday.

Lubbers, Bernie. 2011. *Bourbon Whiskey: Our Native Spirit*. Indianapolis, IN: Blue River Press.

Noe, Fred, with Jim Kokoris. 2012. *Beam, Straight Up: The Bold Story of the First Family of Bourbon*. Hoboken, NJ: John Wiley & Sons.

Okrent, Daniel. 2010. *Last Call: The Rise and Fall of Prohibition*. New York: Scribner.

Thomas, Jerry. 1862. *Bartenders Guide: How to Mix Drinks*. New York: Dick & Fitzgerald.

Toczko, David. 2012. *The Ambassador of Bourbon: Maker's Mark and the Rebirth of America's Native Spirit*. Morley, MO: Acclaim Press.

Veach, Michael R. 2013. *Kentucky Bourbon Whiskey: An American Heritage*. Lexington, KY: University Press of Kentucky.

Young, Al. 2010. *Four Roses: The Return of a Whiskey Legend*. Louisville, KY: Butler Books.

Library of Congress Cataloging-in-Publication Data
Rothbaum, Noah, author.
 The art of American whiskey : a visual history of the
nation's most storied spirit, through 100 iconic labels /
Noah Rothbaum.
    pages cm
Includes bibliographical references and index.
1. Whiskey—United States—History. I. Title.
TP605.R68 2015
338.7′663520973—dc23

Hardcover ISBN: 978-1-60774-718-5
eBook ISBN: 978-1-60774-719-2

Printed in China

Design by Betsy Stromberg

10 9 8 7 6 5 4 3 2 1

First Edition